Beginning to Bloom

Flourishing as the Woman God Created You to Be

A Devotional

Kris Brenes

Beginning to Bloom: Flourishing as the Woman God Created You to Be

Copyright © 2022 by Kris Brenes

Published by Sling & Stone Publishing

Unless otherwise noted, all Scripture is taken from the Holy Bible. New International Version ®, NIV ®. Copyright © 1973, 1978, 1984, 2011.

Cover design by Meaghan Mitchell

Library of Congress Control Number: 2021919255
ISBN: 978-0-578-30116-7

Printed in the United States of America

Contents

Foreword

Too often in life, we are celebrated because of how we look, what we own, what we've done, or who we've been associated with. Performance and resume seem to trump character and identity. Image decimates authenticity and perception undermines reality in a scary era of social media. What should we believe? How should we respond? Enter BEGINNING TO BLOOM, a gem written for such a time as this.

Author Kris Brenes peels away the cool filter of camouflage by humbly sharing the journey of her own life by taking us on a journey through life's most defining themes. She does so not at surface levels but at the deepest level of the human soul while including her family in the narrative. Through the lens of scripture, we are taught to courageously experience reality while embracing God's amazing grace and endless mercy.

For over 25 years, Kris and her family of seven (including five, count them, five children at a time most have just two) have walked through some of life's biggest challenges. They have moved countless times, lived in multiple cities, had to adapt to multiple cultures, driven through life-threatening storms, overcome dysfunctional environments, and survived life-threatening episodes.

You will laugh. You may cry. But one thing is for sure: you will be encouraged. Emboldened even to take life on being assured of the Lord's presence and power at every step and in every season. Past fears can become redemptive pathways to the abundant life Jesus promised, and past failures can become the fuel for defining victories.

Kris writes with articulate simplicity, beautiful style and unique humility. Therefore, this is a book not only to be avidly read for oneself but also to be enthusiastically shared with others. So read on. Let the journey begin. And invite others to join in.

Norman Nakanishi
Pastor, Pearlside Church
Member, Oversight Team, Every Nation Churches

Introduction

I'm not much of a gardener. In fact, even using the word, "much" would be considered an exaggeration. I don't garden, and I have a ZERO percent success rate keeping plants alive.

As a result, I don't have an herb garden or flower bed. I keep only artificial plants in my office, and during Covid, when everyone was kneading bread and digging in the soil, I opted for the former.

In a home filled with growing kids, two dogs, and a cat, the thought of having the responsibility of keeping one more thing alive is just…too…exhausting.

Yet, I'm continually drawn to how scripture references fruit and foliage to illustrate a flourishing life. One of my favorite passages is found in the book of Jeremiah.

Jeremiah is an Old Testament prophet who spoke to the nation of Judah. God was using Jeremiah to address the Jewish people about their continued tendency to look to other things and people as substitutes for their relationship with God. (Sound familiar?)

The Jewish people were seeing life as they knew it slipping away. Babylon was rising in power, threatening to destroy Jerusalem. Families living in Judah were being deported, separated from each other, and exiled to a foreign land. During much uncertainty, Jeremiah gives them insight into how to live a flourishing life amidst desolate and desperate circumstances.

"But blessed are those who trust in the Lord and have made the Lord their hope and confidence. ⁸ They are like trees planted along a riverbank, with roots that reach deep into the water. Such trees are not bothered by the heat or worried by long months of drought. Their leaves stay green, and they never stop producing fruit." Jeremiah 17:7-8 NLT

After a couple of years of Covid lockdowns, quarantines, and social, financial, and political turmoil, doesn't that sound lovely?

This illustration is the modern-day equivalent of an unlimited bank account, a mango tree that is always full of fruit and great surf every day with glassy conditions and light trades. The picture is one of endless supply that never runs out.

Jeremiah is encouraging the Jewish people that although they're experiencing hardships, he is reminding them that desolation is not God's desired destination for them.

Desolation is not God's desired destination for you either. Desolation is not how God created you to live. The desert doesn't have to be where you give up, wither up and die.

But how do we move forward when our lives are filled with everything but the flourishing life of God?

What does it even look like to have a flourishing life?

Even more important, how can we have a flourishing life when the environment isn't ideal for growth and health?

There will be seasons when the heat is turned up, the refreshing rain is sparse, and our lives seem dry.

Even then, you can flourish. In those moments of desolation, God can cause your life to flourish. I'm praying this short devotional will help you take steps in this direction.

I've been there. Gregg and I have five children, and when we started on this parenting adventure over twenty-seven years ago, I was energetic and ready to conquer the world. Yet as the years went by, I began settling for a comfortable life instead of fighting for a flourishing life.

Rarely does our life follow our neatly organized plan. And as an Enneagram 7, Type-A, DISC I/D personality, I had great plans. But having babies, sleepless nights, chasing toddlers, countless moves, and various mom and ministry roles had brought me to a place where I was weary and depleted. While each 'role' was a part of who I was and what I did, none fully satisfied me because they were never meant to. I had to find it in Someone else.

Then came a day when it caught up with me. I started having anxiety attacks, accompanied by months of insomnia, and living with gripping fear. As much as I determined to push through, I felt helpless, which led to guilt and shame and more fear that my life would never be "normal" again.

I went to God's Word for direction, much like I had done every day for many years. But this time, I went with a new desperation. Pleading with Him in prayer, I asked God to reshape my thinking and remold my identity. I surrendered to God every lie, every wound, every attitude, and asked Him to show me truth - His Truth.

What began as a quest for healing led me to something much better. I discovered the richness and faithfulness of Jesus in ways I can't explain. In the fire, God forged my faith. I found Christ right beside me, walking with me through the darkness, providing me with just enough light to take another step.

Not only did my journey eventually produce freedom, but it also brought forth these thoughts you'll read on the following pages. Beginning with every lie, every false motive, every attack on my identity, I dug deep into God's Word for the refreshing treasures of Truth, which are abundant if you're willing to get your hands dirty.

Dear friend, desolation is not God's desired destination for you. So, roll up your sleeves! Let's dig our lives deep into God's Word and allow His Spirit to refresh us and shape us into the flourishing women God created us to be.

Warmest aloha,
Kris

1

Beginning to Bloom

Day 1 – My Parking Lot Meltdown

Our family had just moved cross-country from Los Angeles, California to Nashville, Tennessee, driving through rain, sleet, and snow with five children under ten years old, in a packed minivan with a pet bunny. Whew!

After one month on the road, eating way too much fast food, and living out of various hotels, everyone in the family (including the bunny) had frazzled nerves, testy tempers, and fragile emotions.

To escape the cramped quarters of our hotel room (yes, ALL

seven of us were staying in ONE room, *including* the bunny), one night we thought we'd eat at one of our favorite restaurants. I have no idea why we dared to venture to a semi-nice restaurant at this point of the trip – clearly, we were borderline delirious.

Your family has probably *never* had this kind of experience, but at the risk of being vulnerable – my pain will now become your pain.

Our three boys conveniently chose to expend an entire month's worth of energy during this one-hour restaurant break, making LOTS of noise, bouncing up and down in the booth where we were sitting, wrestling, arguing… you get the picture. As I was getting the "stink eye" from other restaurant patrons, our one-year-old daughter conveniently chose this moment to produce her own "stink" in the form of a toxic poopy diaper.

Yes, we were THAT family.

On the verge of tears, I ventured into the bitter cold to scrounge the floor of our minivan, hoping to find a diaper hidden amidst piles of toys, luggage, and fast-food trash. My husband, Gregg, handed me the keys and, in an exasperated tone, expressed the weariness of the last month by saying, *"If you don't come back, I understand."*

We laugh about it now, but at the moment, we were questioning our decision to uproot our family from a comfortable house, stable job, and close friends to venture into this unknown territory of big belt buckles and country music.

This wasn't what we had signed up for. The picture didn't look as glamorous as we thought it would. In fact, it didn't look appealing at all. It would have been easy to give up and go back to what was familiar. This was difficult.

Tiring.

Painful.

Lonely.

Uncomfortable.

As a little girl, I remember having lofty aspirations and dreams of what I would someday become. I had big plans to change the world and high hopes for what God would someday use me to accomplish.

Yet, that stormy night, I unexpectedly found myself in the middle of a snowy parking lot in an unfamiliar town, scouring my incredibly messy minivan for a clean diaper while my other four kids wreaked havoc in a neighborhood restaurant.

Did God forget that I have a *college education*?

What happened to my plans to *be* different and my aspirations to *make* a difference? What happened to my youthful passion and determination?

I was weary. I was tired. I was just trying to keep my head above water. I was overwhelmed by the unrelenting waves of change that had swept through our family in the last six months.

As a result, even the wonderful things around me, like my family and this great new opportunity, lacked luster, and everything seemed like *so…much…work.*

Perhaps you can relate. Maybe you're tired. That precious new baby you so desperately love has left you sleep-deprived and feeling overwhelmed.

Your job has become the same old routine, and you're just going through the motions week after week.

Or perhaps you're in a season where you feel sidelined, left out, or overlooked by God, wondering what you can contribute?

Maybe you're trying to find your place amid change and transition.

You feel stuck. You long for more.

Thinking maybe somewhere along the line, you missed your opportunity? Or maybe that your mistakes have disqualified you?

You're not alone.

In fact, throughout the scriptures, we see many God-followers wonder some of the same things.

Consider the love and tenderness God expressed to his children through the prophet Isaiah… *"But Zion said, 'The Lord has forsaken me, the Lord has forgotten me.' 'Can a mother forget the baby at her breast and have no compassion on the child she has borne? Though she may forget, I will not forget you! See, I have engraved you on the palms of my hands; your walls are ever before me.'"* Isaiah 49:14-16

As God tenderly reassures the nation of Israel, God persistently affirms His love for us, continually reminding us of

His loving care and faithfulness.

Gently, He prods us to remember to look to Him.

God has not forgotten you. He created you, knows you intimately, and has a great plan for your life – one that will bring glory to His name. As you seek Him and allow your life to be shaped by Him in an increasingly greater way, He will show you the next step to take.

Things may not always turn out the way you expected, and you may find yourself trapped in a restaurant during a winter storm with energetic toddlers, but you can trust that He is good, He hasn't forgotten you, and He will lead you every step of the way.

Day 2 – Times They are a-Changin'

My meltdown years ago in that snowy Nashville parking lot wasn't the only time I've struggled as a mom to grasp my identity. Still, after twenty-nine years of marriage and motherhood, I encounter circumstances that rattle me and expose fears, insecurities, and weaknesses I didn't even know I had.

You know the feeling. It's that turning you get in your stomach when you…

- Start a new job
- Move to a new city
- Send a child off to college

- Walk through unforeseen health issues
- Navigate an unexpected divorce
- Adjust as a growing family

When I find myself getting that uneasy feeling, I've found it helpful to remind myself to place my identity and security in the right place.

The temptation for me is to fix my hope on things that are comfortable, predictable, and familiar. When those aren't there anymore, the little things that shouldn't bother me illicit a bigger reaction than they warrant.

Like when our family went to a drive-through fast-food chicken place and they were out of chicken. Seriously?! How does this even happen?! But it really should NEVER happen to a sleep-deprived mom of a newborn. Just sayin'. (Apologies to the worker who just happened to be the bearer of bad news.)

Perhaps right now, you're finding yourself in an unexpected place where the sand is shifting beneath your feet, and things as you know them are changing, uncertain, unstable.

Dear friend, there is a God who desperately loves you and has so much more for you than you could ever imagine for yourself. He created you to experience a life that is rich, purposeful, and fulfilling. And He is faithful to walk you through whatever you're facing.

God desires to give you something better than a neat, nicely coiffed, comfortable life. He offers you something stronger to anchor yourself to.

Something stable.

Something unchanging, sustaining, and incredibly fulfilling.

In the book of Ephesians, we see a man named Paul praying for his friends in the town of Ephesus. It's one of my favorite scripture passages and it's my prayer for you as well.

Let's read Paul's words to the Ephesians, "*When I think of all this, I fall to my knees and pray to the Father, [15] the Creator of everything in heaven and on earth. [16] I pray that from his glorious, unlimited resources he will empower you with inner strength through his Spirit. [17] Then Christ will make his home in your hearts as you trust in him. Your roots will grow down into God's love and keep you strong. [18] And may you have the power to understand, as all God's people should, how wide, how long, how high, and how deep his love is. [19] May you experience the love of Christ, though it is too great to understand fully. Then you will be made complete with all the fullness of life and power that comes from God. [20] Now all glory to God, who is able, through his mighty power at work within us, to accomplish infinitely more than we might ask or think.*" Ephesians 3:14-20 NLT

Write this on an index card. Tape it on your bathroom mirror. Memorize it. Internalize it. Our God can do infinitely more and far beyond what we can ask or think.

Every good thing that you've experienced in your life…God is able to do more.

Every difficult thing you've faced, God, in His infinite goodness and unlimited resources, can use and redeem it for His purpose.

Every dream that you can imagine for your life…God is able to do more.

Everything that is beyond your ability to control, comprehend, understand, or imagine – God is able to do more than that too.

Paul is struggling in such a great way to describe this concept that theologian Charles Spurgeon noted that Paul constructed an expression that is entirely his own. "No language was powerful enough. He is able to do exceedingly abundantly, so abundantly that it exceeds measure and description."[1]

God can do *infinitely more* through our lives than we can imagine. We don't have to wait to experience His power in a few years when we get our life together. He has the power and ability to do whatever He desires when He desires to do it.

This includes His plan for YOUR life. Regardless of your circumstances, despite how hopeless they seem, God can bring healing and restoration and do more than you could ever imagine.

However, I believe we often miss the most crucial part of tapping into this *infinitely more* awesomeness that God has for us.

It's a partnership with Him (see verses 16-17)!

I pray as you go through these short devotions, you will come to know the immensity of God's love for you, you will be filled with the fullness of God, and you will believe that God, through His power, is able and willing to do *infinitely more* in your life than you could ever imagine.

Take a courageous step and let go of the insecurities, fears, and weaknesses holding you back and replace them with the *infinitely more* presence and power of God.

Day 3 – Time to Bloom

Our move to Nashville was uncomfortable and inconvenient. But we adjusted, planted roots, made friends, and loved living there...for two years.

Then, we moved again.

This time over 5,000 miles away to Hawaii. A beautiful island deep in the Pacific, more than 2,000 miles from the mainland.

Fun fact: Hawaii is the most isolated, populated landmass in the world. *Y'all*, we are literally in the deep, deep South and the far, far West, *brah*.

I left friends...again. Left family...again. Didn't have anything familiar to comfort me...again.

Had to adjust to a new culture and find new schools, new friends, new sports leagues, a new grocery store, a new hairstylist, and new doctors…again.

Even more challenging, *our kids* left friends, schools, youth groups, and sports teams…again.

And once again, God gently began to unearth – like a shovel tilling soil – the areas in my life where I was looking to the wrong things for my identity and security.

It's hard to see with a long-term perspective when you're hurting and steeped in less-than-desirable circumstances. But through the years, I've come to realize God will always use the shaking, stirring, chipping, and molding in my life to build something special. To build something in my life that is of greater worth. Something that will bring God glory and be a blessing to others.

If I surrender to Him.

As much as God wants to build something beautiful in my life, His work is limited by my lack of cooperation when I exert all my energy to grasp and control, resist and oppose.

You see, God wants to do something *in you* so He can do something even greater *through you*. As a sculptor chips away at a marble slab to unveil something beautiful hidden within the marble, God will chip, mold, and shape your life to unveil the true beauty of who He created you to be.

Even in the pain.

Even in the loneliness.

Even in the loss.

Even in the uncertainty.

Your story is unique. Your personality and gifts are like no one else's. The Bible calls you God's workmanship. His masterpiece.

Check out Ephesians 2:10 and catch a glimpse of how God sees you. (This is a good one to write down and memorize.)

Paul writes, *"For we are God's handiwork, created in Christ Jesus to do good works, which God prepared in advance for us to do."* Ephesians 2:10

YOU are God's handiwork, His workmanship. He created you for a specific purpose. All your difficulties, all your challenges, all your struggles can be used for God's greater purpose. God has an amazing ability to use your everyday life to display His love and power to the world.

Oftentimes, the temptation is to desperately search for what's missing in our lives and lose sight of what we have been given – the blessings and gifts that are right in front of us!

In an attempt to rekindle our zest for life and purpose, we go searching for it elsewhere.

We think, *"Perhaps I should get a new job or career?"*

Or, *"Maybe things will be different if I move to a new city, get into a new relationship or make new friends?"*

Or possibly, *"Should I try a new school or get a new hobby?"*

And sometimes, this helps. But most of the time, after a while, the same problems turn up there, too. Because the real challenge is not so much the circumstances around us. The real challenge is often because of something within us.

In moments of confusion, discouragement, monotony, and uncertainty, it's easy for us to look at the wrong things, the wrong people, and the wrong places for worth and value.

But what would happen if, instead of trying to fix our problems by changing our circumstances, we allowed God to change us? What if we surrendered to Him and asked Him to mold us into the women He created us to be?

What would it look like for you to anchor your identity in Christ?

You are of great worth to God. His masterpiece. Don't doubt that. In the routine of life, God has a beautiful treasure for you. In your everyday activities, He desires for you to live fulfilled and satisfied. Through the dark and difficult times, He has made His peace and grace available to you.

In his book, *The Life of the Beloved,* Henri Nouwen writes, "The spiritual life is not simply a way of being, but also a way of becoming."[2]

God wants to rekindle your passion for life, not by necessarily changing your circumstances, surroundings, or physical appearance, but by slowly, gently, graciously changing *you.* It's time to bloom!

Day 4 – I'm Tired, Hungry and Wanna Go Home

When I'm tired, stressed, or hungry (or, Lord forbid, a combination of all three!) the road to crazy is a short one. I complain more and become less patient, quick-tempered, and increasingly frustrated. In other words, watch out! Instead of seeing life clearly and through a grateful, hope-filled lens, all I see are the problems I'm facing and my insufficiency to solve them.

Perhaps this is what happened to the Israelites when we find them in Numbers 11. The chapter opens on a less-than-positive note, *"Now the people complained about their hardships in the hearing of the Lord..."* Numbers 11:1a

Life in the wilderness was hard. It was hot. They were tired. They were thirsty. They missed their comfy bed and favorite food.

Perhaps they wondered, "Why did God choose this guy, Moses, to be our leader anyway? I mean, what does *he* know about our people? He was raised in Pharaoh's home and then spent forty years in Midian! Why should we listen to what he has to say?"

Keep in mind, this was only three days into their march from Mount Sinai toward the Promised Land.

THREE DAYS, PEOPLE!

In the year since the Israelites had left Egypt, they had seen and experienced God's dramatic deliverance (Exodus 14). They had received his miraculous provision of manna (Exodus 16). God had given them water from a rock (Exodus 17), and if that wasn't sufficient to bolster their faith, they witnessed His presence daily, leading them in the form of a cloud by day and a pillar of fire by night (Numbers 10).

Wasn't that enough to keep the pep in their step and hope in their heart? Wasn't their freedom enough to fuel their faith to find joy in their journey?

Apparently not.

Complaining was their "go-to" move when things became hard (see Exodus 15:24, 16:2; 17:3, Numbers 14:2, 16:11, 41).

They complained. They muttered and moaned. They grumbled and griped. About *everything*.

As the book of Numbers describes it, *"The rabble with them began to crave other food, and again the Israelites started wailing and said, "If only we had meat to eat! ⁵ We remember the fish we ate in Egypt at no cost—also the cucumbers, melons, leeks, onions and garlic. ⁶ But now we have lost our appetite; we never see anything but this manna!"* Numbers 11:4-6

Did they forget what life was like for them in Egypt? It's not like they were livin' the easy life on their beach-front property, with a fully stocked fridge and a Starbucks on every corner!

Did they forget they were *slaves* in Egypt? Did they remember how hard they worked laboring *day and night*? Did they remember what their former leader, *Pharaoh*, was like?

It's easy to let our perspective to become clouded, isn't it? Like a dull film settling on my contacts, I, too, find myself navigating with compromised vision. Instead of looking at all the good that surrounds me, I find myself focusing on the negative and – gasp –complaining.

Maybe you can identify. My days are probably a lot like yours—working, taking care of my kids, making meals, cleaning house, doing laundry, helping kids with homework, driving back and forth between school and sporting events. Repeat.

I can easily lose sight of the bigger picture. Slowly, my energetic, faith-infused, hope-filled heart wanes and my outlook on life begins to seem so . . . blah.

Usually, about that point, I'll go on Facebook or Instagram and all my feelings are confirmed – I'm reminded of how ordinary my life is compared to everyone else's.

And subtlety, I'm in a downward spiral into a cycle of complaining and self-pity.

I hate to admit it, and I'm good at justifying it, making excuses for it, and minimizing it.

But look at how God responds to the Israelites' complaining, *"...and when he [the Lord] heard them his anger was aroused. Then fire from the Lord burned among them and consumed some of the outskirts of the camp."* Numbers 11:1b

Yikes. That's pretty serious stuff.

God heard their complaints, and He wasn't very happy about it. This verse tells us that God was so angry that He sent fire to consume some of them.

Isn't that a little extreme? Or as my kids would say, a little *"extra"*?

But it's worth seriously considering: if God's anger was aroused when the Israelites complained, how would he respond to *me?* To my grumbling, my complaining, my lack of gratitude?

You see, when we respond to God's work in our life with a complaining attitude, we're intimating that what God has given us is insufficient.

Like a toddler throwing a tantrum, we demand something more, something different, *something we feel we* deserve. Our whining and stomping call into question God's provision.

And God hates it.

What if we learned to pause? To express gratitude. To thank God for creating me and making me *just as I am*, with all my flaws and inconsistencies.

I believe that's the path to experiencing God's deep contentment and peace in my soul. That's the first step for us to take as we embrace who God has created us to be. When we learn to express gratitude for the little things, the little things don't seem so ordinary anymore. They're seen as gifts given to us by a good and gracious Father.

And then something even crazier begins to happen. Our heart begins to change. Our perspective begins to change. We walk lighter and freer because we're not looking around at all the things we wish we had or things we want to change or the things we don't like about ourselves.

We're content.

Even in the hot, dry desert. Even when we're tired. Even when our life doesn't make sense and things aren't working out as we hoped or planned.

We're content because our focus has shifted from inward at our lack to outward at the greatness and goodness of God.

While everything around us demands we get our "outside life" together, God desires to do a much deeper work – one that works from the inside out. And it starts by thanking God for making you just the way you are.

Day 5 – Mirror, Mirror on the Wall…

When our girls were little, they loved watching the movie *Snow White*.

In the movie, Snow White's stepmother, the evil queen, feels threatened by Snow White's beauty. Every morning the queen would ask her magic mirror, *"Mirror, mirror on the wall, who's the fairest one of all?"*

Every day the mirror responded in a way that pleased the queen and affirmed her beauty.

Until one day.

One day the affirmation from the mirror didn't come. There

was now someone in the land considered to be more beautiful than the queen.

The mirror candidly replied, *"You, my queen, have beauty rare, but Snow White is beyond compare."*

The witch's anger, fear, and insecurity manifested in a tirade of emotion as she vowed to get vengeance on her competition.

While the witch desperately craved the affirmation of her beauty and approval of her worth, I can't help thinking that we, as women, aren't much different.

How often do I "go to the mirror" to measure my worth? My identity? My looks? My weight? To see how my clothes fit? To stare in horror at the gray hair and wrinkles that seem to be multiplying by the day?

How often do I look to others to build my confidence and affirm my significance? Seeking their approval, desiring their compliments?

How often do I search for value and meaning through my work? Working with messed-up motives to fill some void in my life? Avoiding situations where I may fail or look bad?

How much of my life have I invested in trying to secure the approval of others? Avoiding conflict, acquiescing, and people-pleasing because I don't have the self-confidence to assert myself?

Ouch. Too much.

And then, sometimes, when things don't work out as I had hoped, I respond with the same childlike behavior as the witch! I become angry and defensive, feeling rejected, anxious, and discouraged.

Poor me. *sigh*

We all have an inborn desire and need for worth and significance. God created us that way.

We invest a lot of time taking care of the externals but sometimes fall short when it comes to investing in the internals – our true selves. Gradually, we find ourselves sinking in the rut of *not enough*.

Not smart enough, not pretty enough, not thin enough, not young enough, not old enough, not successful enough, not good enough, not enough as a mom, not enough as a wife, not patient enough, not kind enough...

We can fill our lives with a lot of good things – career, marriage, children, friendships, and success, but none of it will permanently fill that nagging cry for worth and significance.

None will be enough.

Read how the apostle Paul inspired the Corinthian people in their quest for worth and significance, *"We are confident of all this because of our great trust in God through Christ. [5] It is not that we think we are qualified to do anything on our own. Our qualification comes from God."* 2 Corinthians 3:4-5 NLT

Only God gives us reason to be confident. Only God qualifies us. Only God can eternally fill the void, and only God can fully satisfy. Our worth is completely in Christ alone.

When we look to other people and other things to define our worth, we miss out on being able to embrace the uniqueness of who God has made us to be.

When we scramble to fill our need for worth and significance with people and our performance, we miss out on being filled with the fullness of God.

Depending on your job, husband, children, friends, success in school, or anything else for satisfaction will only leave you longing for more. There will always be someone more qualified, more talented, kinder, funnier, smarter, prettier . . . more perfect!

Trust me, it will drive you crazy.

Your faith and hope aren't anchored in your circumstances. They're not rooted in your relationships. They're not built on the foundation of what you can do.

They're anchored in Jesus and His power to radically transform and completely fulfill your life. Embracing our identity in Christ empowers us to live differently – to bloom and flourish as the woman He created us to be.

My prayer for you is that during our time together, God would affirm His love for you and as you meditate on the scriptures, God would reveal to you, in a greater way, how He sees you and how He created you to live.

2

An Issue of Identity

Day 1 – Bless this Mess

Our first home! We skimped, saved, and shifted money around to make it happen.

Even more exciting – this home was brand new. I was able to pick the carpet, paint, light fixtures – everything! (At least everything I could squeeze into our small starter home budget.)

Nearly every day, we visited our soon-to-be home. We walked on the foundation slab. We wrote scriptures on the walls and frames. We discussed, deliberated, and debated over countertops, carpet, and colors.

It was almost finished.

The builders just needed to add the final touches, install the lights, and hang the doors in the bedrooms. As we walked through our future home, dreaming of the family memories we would someday make within these walls, we noticed that one of the bedroom doors wouldn't completely shut.

We pulled and pushed, jimmied, and jammed, but it *just wouldn't budge.*

Gregg called the contractor and told him our dilemma, to which the contractor replied, "It's fine. Don't worry."

Really?

Not one to let something like this slide, Gregg kindly countered, "I don't think the wall is straight."

Based on the contractor's response, I don't think he liked having his work called into question. The contractor pushed back, hauling out some of his fancy tools to prove the straightness of his structure and the quality of his construction.

Gregg pressed a little more, "Try another wall." He and the contractor proceeded to walk through the entire house, going wall to wall in search of the faulty area, which eventually led them outside our house.

Our *brick* house.

It turns out the entire foundation of the home was slightly slanted. Because of this, one side of the brick exterior was also slanted when they erected the brick exterior. This slight miscalculation threw off the integrity of the whole house.

If you've spent any time watching HGTV, you understand the dangers of building upon a faulty foundation.

I've witnessed Chip break the news to Joanna about dangers he discovered beneath hardwood and drywall.

I've watched the *Property Brothers* renovation budget blown to bits from an unexpected find in the foundation.

They had to fix it. So they went to work...tearing down brick and rebuilding the wall to code. I must add that because this was a super simple starter home on a very small budget, the company did just enough to get it to code. They didn't tear the whole side of the house down and they didn't repair the foundation.

My point in sharing this story with you is...

Sometimes, if we're honest with ourselves, isn't this how we live? How we attempt to navigate life?

Doing just enough to keep our lives afloat. Just enough to look good so no one sees our pain. Just enough to get by.

We adjust, adapt, patch, paint, coat, and cover the cracks and misalignments in our souls.

But the problem in doing this is it denies the reality: If the foundation is faulty, the stability of the whole structure is compromised.

This foundation is your identity.

And one day, with just a little extra pressure on an unexpected area, the weak point will cave, revealing the fractures and fissures as life as you know it comes tumbling down.

Your identity drives how you live. A broken identity will negatively affect your whole life. It will affect your relationship with God and how you interact with others.

And unless you do the hard work of tearing apart what's broken, you can't move forward to live the life God intended.

If your identity is broken, your life is broken.

A broken identity will...

- Steal your confidence.
- Destroy your self-worth.
- Hinder your ability to make decisions.
- Keep you from moving forward to fulfill the life God created you to live.

What are some of the things you cling to as an essential part of your identity? If someone asked you to describe yourself, what would you say? How would you respond?

Through the years, I have described myself as Gregg's wife, Jim and Linda's daughter, Jennifer's sister, a student, a campus missionary, a pastor's wife, and Rebecca, Brandon, Justin, Jordan, and Jessica's mother.

In 1 John 3:1, John is encouraging Christ-followers to see themselves in a different light, *"See what great love the Father has lavished on us, that we should be called children of God! And that is what we are! The reason the world does not know us is that it did not know him."* 1 John 3:1

You don't have to create your identity. You don't have to search the internet to discover it.

You are a child of God. Lavished in great love by a good Father. That is who you are and how God sees you.

You are not identified by what people say about you. You are not defined by your accomplishments or the people you associate with. You are not "a failure", "hopeless", "ugly", "ordinary", "stupid", "fat", "dysfunctional" ...

You get the picture?

Many of us spend far too much time looking at what we once were, thinking about what we are, and dreaming about what we wish we could be. We allow the memories of our past to haunt us like disturbing video clips from a horror movie.

My friend, that's building on a faulty foundation.

But what if we invested this same amount of time and energy in becoming the person God desires us to be? By building on the foundation of who He says we are by becoming the best version of ourselves?

God has a high calling on your life. He takes great pleasure in using ordinary, everyday people to do amazing things. He sees the incredible value, worth and potential in YOU!

He desires for you to become everything He created you to be, which may involve tearing down some walls—habits, attitudes, and ways of thinking—and that may be a little scary at first.

But in the end, your identity will be built on a solid,

unshakeable foundation that will endure the test of time. And that is completely worth the work and mess of the renovation.

Day 2 – What's Your Name?

Recently, our oldest son, Brandon, asked me, "Mom, why did you and Dad give me a name that means 'a hill covered with broom'?"

We named our child after a prolific weed.

Funny, but I don't recall my Christian *baby name book* informing me about this one! I'm confident the definition in the book was rich with meaning and more profound.

Oops, parent fail.

Names are a funny thing, aren't they? They're given to us at birth, and we have no say in the deal. But our name shapes us, defines us, and gives us worth in so many ways.

As a child, I wanted to be named Katie. Anytime we played school or house with the neighborhood kids, I wanted to be called Katie. I thought it was the most awesome name in the world.

But my parents named me Kristan – with an "a". Nobody could ever spell my name properly. Even worse, I could never find my name on those cool personalized license plates in the souvenir stores. *Sigh*

There are other "names" we pick up throughout our life. Some names are healthy and affirming, and some are like labels we never can seem to grow out of. Some of these names increase our self-worth, shaping us and molding us into becoming better people, and some of these names scar us and hurt us in the deepest places of our hearts.

They are...

- Names we give ourselves.
- Names other people give us.
- Names that come because of past choices we made.
- Names we've come to believe are true about us.
- Names we've internalized and buried so deep that sometimes we're unaware of their effect on us.

In the Gospel of Luke, we see Jesus interact with a woman who had been given a name by the people in her community. Please take a moment to read the entire interaction from Luke 7:36-50.

When the Pharisee who was hosting the dinner party saw how Jesus interacted with this woman, he said to himself, *"If this man were a prophet, he would know who is touching him and what kind of woman she is—that she is a sinner."* Luke 7:39

While this Pharisee and perhaps the entire community had named this woman "a sinner", Jesus saw her differently. He saw the woman God created her to be. He saw potential and purpose, and He provided an opportunity for her to experience a fresh start.

It's so important for us to allow the right Person to name us. If we allow other people or even our past to name us, it will adversely affect everything – our relationships, our job, our self-worth, and sometimes even our health.

These false names will steal our confidence, destroy our self-worth, hinder our ability to make decisions, and keep us from moving forward in fulfilling the life God created us to live.

As a young mom, the name that continually haunted me was, "I'm not good enough".

- Not good enough as a mom.
- Not good enough as a wife.
- Not good enough as a friend.
- Not good enough at my job.
- Not good enough as a pastor's wife.

And the more I allowed *not good enough* to define me, the more I tried to be *good enough*– to prove to myself that the name I believed was wrong.

Exhausting! I wore myself out trying to be enough. No matter how hard I worked, I still felt like I was constantly falling short – not really from the expectations of others, but from expectations I put on myself.

All because of a name I had given myself.

"Not good enough" affected my confidence and made me insecure. It caused me to avoid situations where I felt vulnerable and might fail.

I worked like crazy trying to be the person I thought everyone wanted me to be, and I was horrible at it.

How about you?

What name do you have that you've yet to break free from?

Perhaps it's a name someone called you, or possibly you gave it to yourself?

Maybe it's a label someone used to define you?

Maybe you're laboring under the guilt or shame of your past and you can't seem to break free from it?

Let me encourage you today…the way God sees you is bigger than your past. His opinion of you is more valuable than the opinion of others.

I hope you will come to see – through God's Word – a God-centered view of YOU!

In his Gospel, the apostle John unveils a new name for us, *"Yet to all who did receive him, to those who believed in his name, he gave the right to become children of God— [13]children born not of natural descent, nor of human decision or a husband's will, but born of God."* John 1:12-13

What's your name? *Child of God.*

Day 3 – Seeing Clearly

My eyesight isn't what it used to be. I wear glasses for distance, but then I can't see when I'm trying to read. I've been avoiding the whole bifocal thing. I'm not ready to admit that I've reached that season of life.

My current solution is to wear my reading glasses over my regular glasses. When I'm at the beach, I put my sunglasses over them both. Keepin' it classy. My kids aren't embarrassed to be seen with me *at all.*

We work hard to adjust our physical vision, but what about our spiritual vision? How much time and energy do we invest in seeing God clearly? How we view God will direct our life, define our identity, determine our values, and many of the decisions we will make. How we see God is intricately related to how we view ourselves.

If we believe God is loving, we will dwell with security that reflects someone who is loved.

If we believe God is forgiving, we will live confidently, not cowering in shame or condemnation.

If we believe God created people with incredible worth and value, we will treat others as well as ourselves in such a way that supports the value and worth God says his children have.

It's so crucial for us to grasp our identity in Christ – not at a "head" level, but a believe-it-with-everything-you-got "heart" level. Your identity cannot be derived from your career, relationships, or material things.

I used to think I could change the landscape around me and expect my "vision" to improve – change my job, get new friends, move to a different city – surely that would fulfill me and give me a greater sense of worth. But it never did.

Eventually, the same longing in my heart would bubble up to the surface.

Only God is the true source of your identity. Your identity in Christ can be described by how God sees you and how He created you to live.

Jesus is the sure, unshakeable foundation upon whom you can build your life and find lasting worth, significance, and fulfillment. And because God created you, He is the only One who has the right to name you and give you purpose and worth.

Deriving your identity from anywhere or anyone else is identity theft – using another identity that is not your own. And living this way will negatively affect your whole life. It will affect your relationship with God, how you see yourself, and how you interact with others. It will steal your confidence and destroy your self-esteem.

The worst part is that living this way will limit you to a life that is less than what God created you to live. It's impossible to move forward into all God has for you if you see yourself as unworthy and undeserving of God's love and goodness.

God didn't create you in the image of your job, your career, your family, or your money. You were created in the image of God.

The very first chapter of the Bible, opens with God speaking, *"Then God said, 'Let us make mankind in our*

image, in our likeness, so that they may rule over the fish in the sea and the birds in the sky, over the livestock and all the wild animals, and over all the creatures that move along the ground.'
[27] *So God created mankind in his own image, in the image of God he created them; male and female he created them."*
Genesis 1:26-27

Seeing yourself as God sees you will enable you to handle change, endure setbacks, deal with failure, and allow you to navigate the ups and downs of life with strength and resilience. Like an anchor tethers your life – stabilizing and strengthening it, regardless of the current's pull surrounding you.

So, get out the Windex and clean the smudges off your lenses! As for me, I may need to get a new pair of glasses.

Day 4 – Worth Every Penny

School starts next week, and as I mourn the end of summer, I'm gearing up for one of my least favorite parenting duties…the seemingly endless stack of parent forms, class fees, and tuition payments.

Don't get me started on the cost of college textbooks. I'm incredulous that one used book my child will use for four months will cost *several hundred dollars*. Really?! These are students surviving on Cup of Noodles! (And with these payments, the parents may be too!)

You discover the value of something when you know the price paid for it. While some college textbooks may be overpriced, I still pay for them because I see the value of the end-product: a college education for my kids.

God paid a high price for you and me. He gave his only Son, Jesus, as a sacrifice for our sins. You have incredible worth to God – not because of what you've done for Him – but because He created you and desires to have a relationship with you.

Sadly, we often don't look to Jesus as our primary source of identity. We go searching... grasping for it in other places. Looking for that thing, that career, that relationship, that job to give us the worth our hearts are desperately longing for.

For years, I derived my worth from what I did. I lived as if my performance was what made me valuable. I would do, do, do...add, add, add, and wear myself out to prove my worth and significance. When I did well, I felt good, but when I failed, I was devastated. It was like running on a treadmill – I was working hard and completely wearing myself out but going nowhere.

We've looked at how the One who created us is the only One with the right to name us. Similarly, the One who created us is the same One who should define our worth. If we're not allowing the truth of God's Word to define us, something else will.

Over the years, I noticed three places I found myself repeatedly but insufficiently looking to for affirmation and worth.

Perhaps you can relate.

- *Looking to the past.*

"Brothers and sisters, I do not consider myself yet to have taken hold of it. But one thing I do: Forgetting what is behind and straining toward what is ahead..." Philippians 3:13

Recounting failures and disappointments with a liturgy of "if only" will wear you out. It is impossible to move forward if we are continually looking back. Instead, we should strain forward to what's ahead. Your worth is not measured by your past failures, experiences, mistakes, or even your past successes and achievements.

While the past makes us who we are today and teaches us valuable lessons, Paul says we are not to dwell on it. Like Paul, we need to "forget" our past and put it where it actually is – behind us – if we're to move forward into all God has for us.

- *Looking to other people.*

"We do not dare to classify or compare ourselves with some who commend themselves. When they measure themselves by themselves and compare themselves with themselves, they are not wise." 2 Corinthians 10:12

When we constantly compare ourselves with others, we'll never be satisfied. If we compare ourselves with people who appear to be more "put together" and successful than us, we'll feel like we're constantly failing and falling short. And if we compare ourselves to people who seem to be worse off than us, we'll be tempted to give in to pride and criticism. It's a NO-win situation!

No matter how hard we study, how diligently we work for a promotion, how many hours we spend trying to be the best wife and mom, how many diets we try, or how long we strive to be accepted, somebody will come along sooner or later who will outdo, outperform and "outlook" you.

Resist the pull to conform to be like everyone else. Your worth is not measured by your appearance, performance, or the approval that other people give you.

- *Listening to lies.*

"...When he [the devil] lies, he speaks his native language, for he is a liar and the father of lies." John 8:44

You have an enemy that loves to whisper lies to you. And how easily we can be persuaded to believe them! It's his native language to spew forth lies and lure us into his web of deception and confusion.

In Revelation 12:10, we see another name for the devil, *"Then I heard a loud voice in heaven say: 'Now have come the salvation and the power and the kingdom of our God, and the authority of his Messiah. For the accuser of our brothers and sisters, who accuses them before our God day and night, has been hurled down.'"* Revelation 12:10

The Hebrew name for satan means accuser! One of his primary goals is to beat you down with accusations of fear, shame, insecurity, inadequacy, and failure. Satan gains power over us as we begin to listen and believe the lies that are constantly spoken to us.

At times, I have found myself investing more time into reasoning with and embracing the lies in my mind instead of replacing them with the truth of God's word.

Such. A. Waste. Of. Time. Slowly, I'm learning.

In Philippians, the apostle Paul instructs us to live with a different focus, *"Finally, brothers and sisters, whatever is true, whatever is noble, whatever is right, whatever is pure, whatever is lovely, whatever is admirable—if anything is excellent or praiseworthy—think about such things."* Philippians 4:8

Making a concerted effort to shift our thoughts away from things that distract and discourage us can be so hard! Our mind naturally drifts towards our past, other people, and lies. Suddenly we find ourselves stuck and can't even begin to find our way out.

Like a car spinning its wheels in the mud, we expend a lot of energy yet are unable to get any traction to move forward. Moving forward requires us to embrace and focus on things that are true and then discard our old ways of thinking.

The Bible provides us with the foundation of truth on which we can firmly ground our lives. God's Word gives us the strength and traction to move forward when we feel stuck.

My friend, you are a child of God. Your identity and worth are determined by God, not by the people and circumstances surrounding you. Don't settle for anything less!

By looking to our past, we can quickly become defeated, by comparing ourselves to others we can be discouraged. And by listening to the devil's accusations, we can become confused, distracted, and deceived. Only by looking to Jesus can we truly become all God created us to be.

And as a 19th-century philosopher, Soren Kierkegaard, once said, "Now, with God's help, I shall become myself."[1]

Day 5 – My Issues with the Grocery Store Lady

A few of years ago, while on a quick trip to the grocery store, the cashier asked me if I would like to take advantage of their senior citizen's discount.

ARE YOU KIDDING ME?!?!?!?!

Stunned and shocked, I thought perhaps I hadn't heard her correctly – or maybe she was addressing someone else – so I clarified by asking her to repeat what she said. (Thinking…hoping…praying I hadn't heard her correctly. Or maybe her question was intended for the visibly older person behind me?)

She confidently repeated her question as she gazed directly at me. I mustered a futile attempt to mask the wide range of emotions raging through my mind and body as I completed my transaction and quickly exited the store.

While I'm not a *spring chicken*, I'd like to think I don't look "senior" age, and this happened when I was in my late forties, which made it even more offensive!

I was hurt. Appalled. Offended. Angry. Incredulous.

And a part of me wanted to educate her on the finer art of asking appropriate questions.

For example, you should NOT, under ANY circumstances, ever, ever, EVER ask two general kinds of questions:

- Any questions related to a woman's age, and
- Anything that has to do with being pregnant, possibly pregnant, or postpartum baby weight.

If this is your first time hearing this, you're welcome. You have just been spared much embarrassment, ire, and shame.

I went home to complain and cry to my husband and kids, who immediately responded with...

"Did you get the discount?"

Really?!

The next day, in a well-intended attempt to repair my injured self-esteem, Gregg took me to Longs and invited me to purchase whatever beauty/hair/makeup products I desired. What a great husband.

Interestingly, there was one emotion that I didn't expect to find triggered by this incident.

Insecurity.

For the next week or so, I found myself spending an inordinate amount of time comparing my looks, my hair, my skin, my body with other women.

I know it's shallow and shouldn't have bothered me. I know I should be mature enough to just laugh it off.

But it did bother me.

I don't think I'm alone in feeling this either.

Just a glance at the magazine covers in the line at the grocery store and you'll notice how our culture sends plenty of messages about the value of achieving success and attaining "outer" beauty.

Whether it's the latest anti-aging cream, weight loss plan, or hair product, we're seduced to invest a lot of energy into improving our "outside". But how much attention do we direct toward cultivating and caring for inner beauty?

I love how Peter gently instructs and reminds women where their focus should lie, *"Don't be concerned about the outward beauty of fancy hairstyles, expensive jewelry, or beautiful clothes. You should clothe yourselves instead with the beauty that comes from within, the unfading beauty of a gentle and quiet spirit, which is so precious to God."* 1 Peter 3:3-4 NLT

How quickly we can lose focus. In looking for affirmation from the people around us, we spend a lot of time fixing and upgrading our *outer-selves.*

God looks deeper. He sees our heart. He sees who we're becoming. He sees how he created us to live, and it breaks His heart to see us settle for the superficial second best.

I still color my graying hair. I'm still on the hunt for the best anti-aging cream. And I still haven't been able to bring myself to go through that cashier's line at the grocery store.

But my primary focus is on a different place that looks towards a different result of developing an inner beauty that is precious to God and brings glory to Him.

3

Reflections

Day 1 - Reflections

The Ugly Duckling is one of my favorite children's books. Do you remember it? Let me briefly refresh your memory by summarizing it for you.

Once upon a time, born into a batch of adorable little ducklings, hatched an awkwardly large one. Some might even go so far as to say this little duckling was ugly. Despite his mother's attempt to protect and defend him, the young duckling endured much heckling and harassment from the other ducks until, finally, he couldn't take it anymore, and he ran far, far away.

During this time a beautiful flock of birds captivated his

attention. He secretly wished he had been born with even a hint of the beauty these birds gracefully possessed.

Soon after, winter arrived and brought a cold, miserable, lonely time for the little duckling. When the relief of spring finally came, he saw these beautiful birds again and boldly decided to approach them.

Anticipating the same rejection he experienced in the past, much to his amazement, these birds didn't run away from him or mock him but instead rushed to welcome him.

At that moment, he caught a glimpse of his reflection in the water. He couldn't believe it! No longer was he an ugly duckling, but through the cold, dark, lonely winter, he had been transformed into a beautiful swan!

The swan was now thankful for his past experiences of pain and suffering because they enabled him to appreciate further the beauty he now enjoyed.

Who would have dreamed that such beauty could have been forged from such ugliness? [1]

In many ways, I can identify with this little duckling. Perhaps you can, too?

Possibly you've admired the beauty, poise, and "put-togetherness" you've seen in others but doubted you could experience it for yourself. Maybe it's easier for you to believe God can transform other people's lives, but you're skeptical He would do it for you.

Possibly, you've lived with the harsh inner voice stating your "ugliness" for so long that you're used to it and can't imagine anything different.

Perhaps the pain of your past is so overwhelming you feel stuck and don't even know where to begin to experience freedom.

Let me assure you, transformation is what God does best!

As I look back and see how much change and transformation God has brought forth in my life, I am in awe. Areas of my life that I felt utterly powerless to change—places where I felt hopeless—He has lovingly transformed.

It's a process God continues to work in my life day after day, year after year. It's not always easy, and it's not always pain-free. I'm not the same person I was a year ago and, thankfully, I won't be the same person I am today a year from now.

Although I'm not who I eventually *hope* to be, I thank God that I'm not who I *used* to be.

Sadly from an early age, we begin to believe lies that are subtly sown into our minds and hearts. Even in elementary school, children begin to identify people as "ugly or pretty", "fat or skinny", "smart or not smart", "popular or unpopular", and "valued or unvalued".

As we grow older, these labels continue to shape and mold our identity, influencing the way we see ourselves and other people.

Thoughts such as *"I don't fit in"*, *"I'm unloved"*, *"No one understands me"*, *"No one cares about me"*, or *"I'll always be a failure"* shape how we see ourselves and affect the way we live.

The way we live reflects how we see ourselves.

Proverbs, a collection of wise sayings in the Old Testament, says this, *"As water reflects the face, so one's life reflects the heart."* Proverbs 27:19

What do you think about yourself? When no one's around. No one is watching.

It's just you.

How do you see yourself? How you see yourself reflects what's going on inside your heart. Your heart is your true self – revealing the real you.

How's your heart?

In the heart...that's where the transformation begins.

Day 2 - Beauty from Pain

In the 1930s, the St. Louis Cardinals had a star pitcher who played with youthful personality and passion.

His name was Dizzy Dean.

Dizzy Dean led the St. Louis Cardinals to a World Series title in 1934 when his pitching won them thirty games in one season. Even if you're not a baseball fan, you can appreciate his accomplishment, right?

He was at the peak of his career and seemingly unstoppable until the 1937 All-Star game when a line drive struck him on his foot, fracturing his big toe. Don't underestimate the importance of your big toe, my friends!

Not one to sit on the sidelines, Dizzy found a way to adjust his pitching motion to avoid landing hard on his injured toe. But in the process, he hurt his shoulder, losing his great fastball.

Dizzy Dean's career ended, not because of his broken toe, but because of the shoulder injury he received while compensating for the pain in his toe.[2]

Many of us, perhaps you today, have learned to compensate for injuries to our identity. These injuries are lodged so deep in your heart, and over the years, they've shaped the way you live.

You've learned to compensate. Conceal. Adjust. Adapt.

And something deep inside *just feels off.* It affects how you see yourself, your relationship with God, your relationships with others, how you live, and how you act.

Whether it's due to shameful words, shattered dreams, or painful experiences, these injuries are so deep we often don't even know they're there. We've just become experts at compensating for them.

Somehow, we must find a way to move beyond the discomfort and pain to embrace something far greater. God didn't create us to limp around, masking, covering up, and compensating for our pain. He created us to live differently – with wholeness, vitality, and purpose.

The path to experiencing this begins by allowing His loving presence to change and transform our lives. He's an expert at taking the brokenness of our life and building something beautiful.

In fact, it's what He does best. Paul says it this way, *"Now if we are children, then we are heirs—heirs of God and co-heirs with Christ, if indeed we share in his sufferings in order that we may also share in his glory. [18] I consider that our present sufferings are not worth comparing with the glory that will be revealed in us."* Romans 8:17-18

The brokenness, the suffering, and the injustice that we see on earth pale compared to the glory we will experience when we meet Jesus face to face. As His children, we can live with a confident hope that rises above all our present pain, fear, struggles, and insecurities because someday, we will share with Jesus in experiencing the complete freedom and wholeness of his eternal kingdom.

The Greek word for glory in the above verse is *dóxa*, which means a most glorious condition. The glory spoken of in this verse relates to us, His children, and refers to the ideal condition in which God created and intended His children to live.[3]

God wants you to become everything He originally meant for you to be. He wants you to embrace your true identity!

Even better news: His glory can begin to be revealed through your life, right here, right now. Even through challenges, even through suffering, you can live in a way that glorifies God by pointing others to the eternal hope that is available in Christ.

The past failures and the present difficulties don't determine our future and can't hinder God's purpose from being accomplished in our lives. Nothing even compares to the glory that God will someday reveal in us—the fullness and completeness of total wholeness, restoration, and freedom.

Amidst great seasons of joy and success, our lives will be checkered with moments of heartache, disappointment, failure, and unfulfilled dreams. God wants to use those seasons of suffering to mold, change and transform us. Ironically, it's often during the most challenging seasons in my life when I've seen God do his greatest work.

If you continue reading the rest of Romans 8, you'll find Paul building on this truth as he writes about an unshakable hope we can have as Christ-followers. One of my favorite verses is verse 28, *"And we know that in all things God works for the good of those who love him, who have been called according to his purpose."* Romans 8:28

All things . . . that includes the financial things, the bad relationship things, the family things, the school things, the depressing things, the past things, the job-related things . . .

You get the idea?

Your number one hurt, your number one problem, God can use to help mold and shape you so you will more accurately reflect the image of His Son and bring glory to Him through your life.

Often, we limit "the good" we're hoping to see in our life to temporal, material things. Much of the time, God desires so much more for us. He looks beyond our circumstances; His perspective extends into eternity and "His good work" usually involves doing something of far greater eternal worth and glory as He works in our hearts.

Whatever you've endured or experienced, it's my prayer you would know God is good, He is faithful, and you can trust Him. He desperately loves you and wants the best for your life. You're beautiful and precious in His sight, and He wants to use your current mess to make something beautiful.

This doesn't mean He's a fairy godmother-type who candy-coats all our problems and pain with fairy dust and rainbows (although that sounds appealing).

It's often quite the contrary. Difficult circumstances can provide a pathway to growth and maturity.

God loves you so much that He desires to work deep in your heart if you let Him. Some of the innermost places of character are forged through pain and suffering. Even the most horrible, ugly experiences can be an opportunity for God to make something beautiful, something good, in your life.

Don't compensate. Don't cover-up. Don't conceal. Don't avoid or ignore. Allow God to do His even greater work of healing in your soul.

Day 3 – Getting a New Outfit

Everyone in our family enjoys spending time at the beach. Thankfully, we live on an island and can go often. In fact, during the summer, my kids go almost every day and sometimes multiple times a day. When my boys were younger, they lived in their board shorts. They wore them to the beach, sometimes to school, while hanging out with friends, and even occasionally to bed!

I had to remind them that just because their board shorts got wet in the ocean *didn't mean they were clean*. There have been times when the several-day-old salty stench on their shorts was unbearable!

While writing to the church in Colossae, Paul uses something as practical as the clothes we wear to illustrate our identity in Christ. No, Paul's not giving us fashion advice. This has nothing to do with fashion week in Milan. Nor is he advocating a particular style of dress.

Paul instructs them, *"But now you must also rid yourselves of all such things as these: anger, rage, malice, slander, and filthy language from your lips. ⁹ Do not lie to each other, since you have taken off your old self with its practices ¹⁰and have put on the new self, which is being renewed in knowledge in the image of its Creator."* Colossians 3:8-10

Paul intimates to those who are following Christ that they need to change their clothes. They must take off the smelly, stinky, dirty clothes of their "old self" and put on some fresh ones – clothes that reflect their new identity in Christ.

Paul doesn't give this as a suggestion; he emphasizes the urgency by telling them to *do this now*. Don't wait for a more convenient time or a better opportunity. Don't justify the stink or try to cover it up by spraying yourself down with Febreeze (yup, I admit I've done that on more than one occasion).

Rid yourself of those behaviors – change your clothes! Don't live like the people around you. Instead, put on a new outfit, a beautiful one purchased with the blood of Jesus, as you strive to look more and more like Him every day. Paul continues this thought through verse 12, *"Therefore, as God's chosen people, holy and dearly loved, clothe yourselves with compassion, kindness, humility, gentleness and patience."* Colossians 3:12

"Chosen...holy and dearly loved."

Right now. As is. This is how God sees you. The real issue for us is this: are we living as if this is true?

Sometimes I've found it easier to believe other people are chosen, holy, and dearly loved than to believe that's how God sees me. We have all fallen short of perfection. We have all blown it. But the good news is God continues to see you as the person He created you to be.

Your identity doesn't come from the things you do or the people around you. It's not earned or worked for. Instead, it's a gift we receive with gratitude from a loving Father.

Paul is telling the Christians in Colossae their identity in Christ should be reflected in how they live and the "clothing" they wear. Their "clothing" should be consistent with their identity.

Our outer life reflects our inward life. As a natural outflow of seeing ourselves as chosen, holy, and dearly loved, we should "clothe ourselves" with compassionate hearts, kindness, humility, gentleness, and patience.

And just as we take off our dirty clothes and put clean ones on, we are to take off attitudes, actions, and things inconsistent with this new identity and clothe ourselves with a holy lifestyle that honors God and accurately reflects who He is.

I love how the NIV Study Bible explains this passage in Colossians 3. Paul is telling the believers, "They are called upon to become in daily experience what they are in Christ."[4]

When we allow God to shape our lives, we begin to see ourselves as the women He created us to be.

He asks us to get rid of some of the "outfits" we've been wearing – to replace them with "clothes" that better represent the God we serve.

When we do this, the transformation not only affects our lives and how we see ourselves, but it also begins to affect how we live. People see Christ in us, and God uses us to influence the community of people around us. Through our lives He displays His love to a broken world!

It's time to get a new wardrobe. Take off the old, worn-out, dirty clothes and ask God to clothe you with His Spirit and His likeness. What an upgrade!

Day 4 - Mirrors

When I was growing up, every year we'd go to the Puyallup Fair (not really, but kinda pronounced, "pull y'all up"). I looked forward to it all year – early release from school, the yummy fair food, the animal and agricultural exhibits (*who will win the biggest pumpkin award this year?*), the sketchy rides…all of it!

One of my annual faves was an attraction called the *Fun House*. Perhaps you've visited one? You enter a building and walk through a maze filled with silly and disorienting things. At some point in the *Fun House*, you enter a room containing a bunch of crazy mirrors. (It was the old-school equivalent of today's Snapchat and Instagram filters.)

I'd run back and forth, giggling as I looked at my warped reflection. Some mirrors would make me look tall and skinny; other mirrors would make me look short and stumpy. But all of them were distortions of reality and didn't accurately reflect how I truly appeared.

If you were to think of your life as a mirror, what do you see in its reflection? Let's be honest, most of us – myself included – would see a reflection that has been terribly warped, clouded, and distorted.

It's time for us to get out some Windex, clean the mirror, change the filter, and do whatever it takes for us to see ourselves as God sees us, through the lens of God's Word – the true, undistorted mirror for our lives.

Because if we're going to get an accurate picture of who we truly are in Christ, if we're going to reflect who Jesus is to a broken world accurately, we need to begin painting a picture of ourselves that resembles who God says we are, right?

As we saw in the last chapter, in Genesis 1, God provides a "frame" for how we should see ourselves, *"So God created mankind in his own image, in the image of God he created them; male and female he created them."* Genesis 1:27

You are created in the image of God.

An image is an accurate representation or reflection of something. So when God says He created us in His image, He means He created us to be like Him and to reflect who He is and what He is like.

This is what distinguishes you and me from everything else that God made. While God made flowers to be like flowers, birds to be like birds, and fish to be like fish, He made us like Himself.

His image is seen in the eyes of the orphaned children in China; His likeness is found among the impoverished in Africa. From the faces of the poor and oppressed to the successful and wealthy, His presence and likeness are found in his children—all of them.

In the movie, *The Help*, one of the main characters, Aibileen, makes an intentional effort to mold the self-image of a little girl. Daily, she has the little girl repeat, *"I is smart. I is kind. I is important."* While the people around her may not affirm the girl's worth, Aibileen is determined to be a positive voice speaking into her heart.

God desires to be this voice in your life. He wants to be the guiding voice shaping your image, molding your character, and defining you.

I love how Bob Goff put it in his book, *Everybody Always*, "God has never looked in your mirror or mine and wished he saw someone else."[5]

If we're not careful, we can find ourselves investing a lot of energy attempting to be who we think we should be or trying to be who others think we should be.

God knows you intimately. Your birth wasn't an accident; it didn't catch God off guard. He planned your life long before you were formed. Before you even took your first breath, He had a wonderful plan for your life. Before you did anything, accomplished anything, or achieved anything, you had value to God simply because He created you.

God speaks to the children of Israel through Isaiah, *"For I will pour water on the thirsty land, and streams on the dry ground; I will pour out my Spirit on your offspring, and my blessing on your*

descendants. [4] They will spring up like grass in a meadow, like poplar trees by flowing streams. [5] Some will say, 'I belong to the Lord'; others will call themselves by the name of Jacob…" Isaiah 44:3-5

You may be thirsting for significance; your hope may have run dry. Your "mirror" may be warped, distorted, or just plain dirty. Time to take off the filters, clean off the mirror, and allow the Word of God to wash over your soul, cleaning you, filling you, shaping you, refreshing you, and molding you into His image. This image gradually comes clearer as you grow in your knowledge of the "Whom" to which you belong.

"What you are is God's gift to you. What you make of yourself is your gift to God."[6] Let's allow God to make us into who He created us to be.

Day 5 - My Life-Long Fixer Upper

One thing I find fascinating about watching home renovation shows is seeing the complete transformation of a house from start to finish.

At first glance, the rundown, outdated appearance seems hopeless. It's hard to imagine any hidden potential beneath the worn, neglected surface. But then, miraculously, in just thirty minutes, a beautiful transformation occurs. The finished product is stunning, and it's hard to believe the beauty hidden within the walls.

God desires to do a similar work of transformation in our lives. He's committed to a life-long renovation project to make us more like His Son, Jesus. It's not something we can do for ourselves, nor does it happen overnight. We are God's life-long, never-ending fixer-upper. And it's a project He delights to do!

Paul describes this work to the church in Corinth. *"Now the Lord is the Spirit, and where the Spirit of the Lord is, there is freedom.[18] And we all, with unveiled face, beholding the glory of the Lord, are being transformed into the same image from one degree of glory to another. For this comes from the Lord who is the Spirit."* 2 Corinthians 3:17-18 ESV

Too many people spend their lives searching for and chasing after things they hope will bring freedom and transformation to their lives.

Here's the Good News! You don't have to look any further. Freedom and transformation are found in Jesus! God loves you so much that He provided a way for you to be truly free – free from the hurts and habits of our past, free from the guilt of previous mistakes, and free from the shame luring us to hide and withdraw.

When we place our trust in Jesus, the Spirit of God begins a work of inward transformation. It's not: try harder, work harder, do more, learn more. It's a freedom we receive from the Spirit of God. What great news!

This verse describes a transformation occurring as we *"behold the glory of the Lord"*. When my children were born, and the doctor placed them in my arms for the very first time, I couldn't stop looking at them.

I *beheld* them.

They captivated my attention and captured my affection. I fixed my eyes on them to observe all their little features and mannerisms. I didn't casually glance at them and ask the nurse to take them; I held them close and gazed upon them. In a moment, my life, attention, and priorities forever changed because I beheld my newborn children.

When God captures our heart, our passion, desires, and focus should also change. We make adjustments to our life because our heart is in a different place with different priorities driving us. We want to be with Him, and we want to be like Him. As we *behold His glory*, His Spirit works in us and changes us.

The word *transformed*, in Greek, is *metamorphóo*, meaning to transfigure or to change one's form.[7]

Perhaps you're familiar with this word as it's the process caterpillars go through when they transform into butterflies. When the caterpillar surrounds itself with a cocoon and later emerges as a beautiful butterfly, no resemblance of the caterpillar remains—it is a complete transformation.

God is at work to completely transform you as well, and you won't look or act the same when He is finished. Christ wants His

61

character and likeness to be expressed in your whole being.

Sin has muddied the waters and clouded the mirror by which we can perfectly reflect God's image. The voice of accusation and lies deafens the still, quiet voice of God's Spirit affirming and shaping us. But by his abundant grace and forgiveness, as we allow Him to unclutter our souls and shine the truth of His word into our hearts, He changes and transforms us to be more like Him.

God loves you too much to leave you the same. He knows that a little pain, a little inconvenience, a little discomfort in time will produce a better you—one that is more like Him.

I figure if I'm heading in the right direction, I'm one tiny step closer every day to being the woman God created me to be.

My friend, you can live with the confidence that God loves you, the security that your relationship with Him doesn't change, and the hope that His transforming power can set you free.

Just take a tiny step towards Him – every day.

Stormie Omartian wrote that it is "when you look into the mirror and see the excellence of Jesus reflected back, that's when you will have a sense of your true worth. The actual transformation takes place every time you worship the Lord for his perfection."[8]

4

You are Forgiven

Day 1 – What I Need the Most

One sunny day several years ago, we piled the surfboards in the car and headed to the North Shore for a family day at the beach. As the day turned to dusk, we decided to stop at one last beach. The waves were perfect for my young kids, who were learning to surf.

This beach consisted of two breaks: a small, gentle inside break and an outside break which was a little more challenging to navigate. We weren't aware that an invisible channel, known to have a powerful current, existed between these two breaks. (This would've been *really* helpful info to have on the front end.)

It was after 4pm when our three oldest children journeyed into the ocean. They were laughing, splashing, and having a lot of fun, that is, until the conditions changed.

Without warning, the skies quickly turned from sunny and serene to overcast and ominous. And as the sun began to set, the waves that had been gentle just minutes before, quickly transformed into powerful waves with a potent current.

The current was so strong it swiftly sucked my kids toward a dangerous rocky area. From the shore, I could see the waves and current batter them, dragging them further and further away!

I leaped into action to do what I do very well – *I panicked and freaked out*. However, yelling at them from the shore wasn't very productive. My kids were stuck and unable to break away from the powerful surf on their own strength.

I enlisted the help of the lifeguards. The lifeguards saw the threat and acted quickly to help, but my kids were so busy having a great time that they were completely unaware of the imminent danger. As the lifeguards paddled out to save them, they were incredulous that I would have the audacity to send someone to rescue them.

In their opinion, they were perfectly fine and had everything under control. Even today, if you were to ask my kids, they would ALL tell you the lifeguards were a nuisance that day.

They would tell you the lifeguards were ruining their fun.

They would tell you that the lifeguards were an inconvenience, interrupting their day at the beach. They would tell you they didn't need to be rescued.

Because they didn't see their need to be saved.

When you don't think you need to be rescued, the idea of a savior is a big "yawn", an annoying nuisance, or maybe even boooooring.

For many people (perhaps this may even be your perspective), this is how they view God. They don't see their need for Him. The whole idea of Christianity and following Jesus is inconvenient, interfering with their lives and ruining their fun.

But for those of us who have experienced the pull of life's current... For those of us who have been beaten by the swell of the waves... For those of us who have been pulled under and tossed around on the ocean shore until we're exhausted and sinking...

We understand *The Story* differently.

We respond to the Savior with gratitude and sobering humility because God came to do for us what we are powerless to do for ourselves. He sent Jesus to rescue us.

As the Gospel of Luke declares, *"I bring you good news that will cause great joy for all the people. [11]Today in the town of David a Savior has been born to you; he is the Messiah, the Lord."* Luke 2:10-11

God sent a Savior. Not a helper, not a life coach, not more rules or rigid expectations.

A Savior.

Until you come to grips with the fact that you need to be rescued, the idea of a Savior is an inconvenience or irritation, as if someone is trying to ruin your good time.

But for those who have truly embraced their brokenness and are conscious of what Jesus truly did for them, the response is much different.

It's not, *"I have to..."* or *"I need to..."*

When we think of Jesus, we experience unfiltered joy and unsolicited devotion. There is an appreciation and gratitude that extends beyond obligation because...

He saved me.

And that, my friend, is good news for all people.

Day 2 – Finding Your Way Home

Years ago, our family was driving home from Atlanta to Nashville, where we were living at the time. Looking at the map (this was back in the *ancient days* before Waze and Google maps when you navigated your road trips using a *paper map*), we found what looked to be an alternate route that would shave a little time off our four-hour drive.

Deciding it was worth the try, we got on the unfamiliar road. However, what the map didn't show us was that this seemingly reliable highway eventually became a small country road that weaved through the desolate backwoods of North Carolina's Smokey Mountains.

As the sun went down, we found ourselves on a lonely path with no town or evidence of life anywhere in sight. We were lost, a little scared, and praying we would find a familiar road before landing as a feature story on a mystery episode of *Dateline*.

In Romans 3:23, Paul tells the Roman people that all have sinned and fallen short of living the way God created them to live. If you've never made a mistake, never uttered a harsh word, or never dragged around a bad attitude, never harbored an impure thought, you are off the hook.

As for the rest of us, we're guilty. All of us have lost our way.

We may have started down the right road with great intentions, but somewhere along the way we wandered off the path, becoming twisted and turned around. And our sin separates us from a holy God.

In this verse, the Greek word for *sin* is *hamartano*, which means to miss the mark (and so not share in the prize), to err, or swerve from the truth. Thayer's Greek Lexicon adds: to be without a share in, to wander from the path of uprightness and honor.[1]

We have all wandered from the path God has for us. Through our sin, our willful disobedience, and our disregard for God and the way He created us to live, our relationship with God has been severed. It's not that God doesn't love us or has turned His back on us, but our sin has destroyed the relationship that God created for us to enjoy with Him.

God is holy and nothing unholy can even stand in His presence. Although we were created to enjoy God, our sin has built an insurmountable gap between God, who is completely holy, and us, who are not. Therefore, the eternal riches, relationship and glory for which God created us to enjoy, we cannot receive with hearts filled with sin.

So what are we to do? How can we find our way back to the road on which God created us to live?

Here's the good news! God doesn't want us to live our life apart from Him. He provided a way for us to experience a relationship with him.

Paul continues explaining God's provision for us, *"You see, at just the right time, when we were still powerless, Christ died for the ungodly. [7] Very rarely will anyone die for a righteous person, though for a good person someone might possibly dare to die. [8] But God demonstrates his own love for us in this: While we were still sinners, Christ died for us."* Romans 5:6-8

When I moved away for college, I had no means on my own to return home: no car, and no money. The price was too costly for me to pay. My parents, because they loved me and wanted to spend time with me, did what I could not do for myself and paid the price for me to come home.

On a far greater scale, God paid the price to bring His children home. God loves you and desires to have a relationship with you so badly that He did for you what you could not do for yourself: He sent His only Son, Jesus, to die on a cross for you.

Jesus lived a perfect, sinless life. He died the death we deserved, paying the price for our sins. After three days, He rose again from the dead proving He is the Son of God, defeating sin and death and offering the gift of salvation and forgiveness of sins to anyone who repents and believes in Him.[2]

Jesus paid the price to take away your sin, so you could come home—so you could enjoy a vibrant relationship with Him and experience the fullness of the life He created you to live.

He is your way home.

Day 3 – The Uninvited Dinner Guest

Imagine you're invited to someone's house—someone you hardly know—and you arrive to find the door open.

As you enter, no one greets you . . . in fact, no one even acknowledges your arrival. No one says hello, no one offers to take your coat, no one offers you anything to drink. How would you feel? What would you do?

In Luke 7, we read about a man who was hosting an intimate dinner party for well-known, well-educated men from the community. It was a special event for the Pharisees, who were among the educated elite and religious leaders during this time.

They had heard of Jesus but had yet to embrace the new ideas He had taught His followers. Yet, for some reason, Simon had invited Jesus to the dinner that evening, and as a visiting rabbi, He would have been regarded as a guest of honor.

However, the arrival of Jesus at the home of Simon was largely ignored. Even the most basic rules of hospitality were disregarded toward Him. No one greeted Him with a kiss (the customary welcome), no water was given for Him to wash his feet (the most minimal rule of hospitality), and no oil was put on His head (an optional but thoughtful gesture towards guests during this time). This wasn't an accident, mistake, or oversight but a deliberate slap in the face, and everybody knew it.[3]

Yet, Jesus proceeded to enter and took His place reclining at the table. The tension mounted as everyone waited to see how He would respond.

It was during this dinner party that an unusual interaction began to unfold. To the astonishment of the host and guests, a woman walked in and approached Jesus while He reclined at the table with the other guests.

Even more shocking was this woman's notorious reputation in the community. Women in ancient Jewish culture didn't hold an honorable place in society, and they were usually not acknowledged or even addressed in public. How much more appalling that *this* woman would somehow feel compelled to come near Jesus!

You are Forgiven

But something was different about her now. She no longer had a seductive air about her; she no longer hung her head in shame. Instead, she radiated joy, peace, humility, and purity that had not been evident in her life for a long time. Something was different. After years of feeling dirty and discarded, she had changed.

This woman knew how it felt to be rejected. She knew what it was like to be ridiculed and shunned. Something inside her demanded that she gives her all to Jesus because He had given so much to her.

Ignoring the cold stares and callous comments, this woman boldly approached Jesus and began to kiss His feet. Imagine the scene!

Before she realized what was happening, a wave of emotion rushed over her, and she began to cry uncontrollably. As her weeping escalated and captivated the attention of everyone in the room, she proceeded to use her hair to wipe her tears off His feet!

The feet of Jesus that were unwashed by Simon upon His arrival are now washed by the tears of a sinful woman. Continuing with her display of gratitude, she took her flask of fragrant perfume and lavishly poured it on His feet. This woman withheld nothing, giving her all to Jesus, emptying herself at His feet.

But why? What would motivate this woman to demonstrate such a display of love and affection towards Jesus?

As I reflect on this passage, I think the reason the reason she responded the way she did is because Jesus gave her what no one else had given her - forgiveness and acceptance.

When no one accepted her, He welcomed her. When no one loved her, He loved her as His daughter. When she was alone, He was her friend. When everyone judged her, He restored her. When everyone else labeled her a "sinner", Jesus gave her a new identity as a child of God.

He valued her not as an object but as a woman created uniquely by God. And when everyone else held her past against her, Jesus forgave her and offered her a fresh start.

Jesus explained it this way, *"I tell you, her sins – and they are many – have been forgiven, so she has shown me much love. But a person who is forgiven a little shows only a little love."* Then Jesus said to the woman, *"Your sins are forgiven."* Luke 7:47-48 NLT.

The Greek word for forgiveness used in verse 47 of this passage is *aphiemi*. It means to send away, to let go free, or to pardon. When someone is issued a pardon in a court of law, their past actions are not held against them. They have been given a clean slate, a fresh start, a new beginning.

The woman in Luke 7 probably had a long list of things she would have done differently. You may, too. The good news is God doesn't want you to live in the past, nor does he want you to live under the guilt of the past in the present.

He has something much better for you. God's forgiveness offers you a fresh start, a clean slate. God's forgiveness enables you to enter the fullness of life God has created for you to enjoy.

Day 4 – Another Uninvited Dinner Guest

If you've ever watched a crime drama, you know that many witnesses can be called during a trial to testify regarding their unique knowledge and perspective of a situation. Each testimony adds another layer of detail and a broader understanding of what happened.

The first four books of the New Testament, called the Gospels, provide us with four different perspectives, four unique vantage points, into the life and ministry of Jesus. Each adds another layer of detail and depth to our understanding of who Jesus is and what He came to do.

In Mark 14:1-5, we read Mark's perspective on another dinner party Jesus attended, which another uninvited guest attended. When you're as popular as Jesus, everyone wants to crash your dinner parties.

The events surrounding this meal were brimming with tension. Conflict is beginning to brew. Behind-your-back conversations are being conducted. Crisis is imminent. And to top it all off, Jesus is starting to talk to His disciples about dying and leaving them.

Jesus' followers are now in full-blown crisis mode, attempting to control the crowd and calm the protesters. You can feel the confusion stirring and the intensity rising, shrouding the future with an unsettling uncertainty.

In Bethany, just a few days earlier, Jesus had raised a man from the dead. Jesus brought Lazarus, who was dead for four days, back to life…in their town (John 11)! Many had witnessed it. And even more people had seen Lazarus walking around town since the miracle happened.

Everyone was talking about it! (Sort of like when popular K-pop groups vacation in Hawaii and post their photos on Instagram.)

Most likely, everyone in the area had heard about Jesus, and people were flocking in droves to meet Him. The commotion was palpable, and the religious rulers were even more determined to kill Jesus before the quickly approaching Passover.

Amidst all the chaos, Jesus attends this dinner party at the home of Simon who Mark also adds is *a leper*. Jesus always seems to find, befriend, and gravitate to the outcasts and marginalized.

During this dinner party, something amazing happens, *"While he was in Bethany, reclining at the table in the home of Simon the Leper, a woman came with an alabaster jar of very expensive perfume, made of pure nard. She broke the jar and poured the perfume on his head. 4 Some of those present were saying indignantly to one another, 'Why this waste of perfume? 5 It could have been sold for more than a year's wages and the money given to the poor.' And they rebuked her harshly."* Mark 14:3-5

This wasn't any cheap perfume you could pick up at Walmart. It was extremely costly, said to be worth about a year's wages. Think about it – the average annual income for an individual in the United States is about $44,000, and this woman poured it like a jug of Gatorade on Jesus' head.

The fragrance was also made of pure nard – a costly ointment used to express acts of devotion. This woman lavishly anointed Jesus, giving it all to Him, emptying herself at His feet.

She gave what was potentially her most valuable possession. And while many saw it as a waste, this woman saw it as an investment. A life broken and poured out in service to Jesus is never wasted.

When you understand the magnitude of your debt and the greatness of God's provision through Jesus, gratitude will flow from a surrendered heart that holds nothing back.

Just a few days later, Jesus would go to the cross, giving His life for this woman's sin. For my sin. For your sin.

At the cross, Jesus held nothing back. He gave it all – His bloodshed, His life poured out in service and complete sacrifice.

Some look at the cross and see it as a waste. Jesus saw it as an investment. Because you're worth it.

Peter explained it like this, *"For Christ also suffered once for sins, the righteous for the unrighteous, to bring you to God."* 1 Peter 3:18

In response, shouldn't we lavishly pour out our lives in service to Him?

Day 5 – Take It Personally

Let's return to Jesus' with Simon and the woman in Luke 7:36-50. Simon's understanding of forgiveness appears to differ from the woman's, doesn't it? It seems Simon saw sin as something other people had to deal with; the woman saw sin as something she was incapable of dealing with on her own.

Sometimes it's easier to recognize the sin, flaws, and shortcomings in others than it is to see them in us, isn't it? Simon was quick to judge others, yet sadly, he did not see his need for repentance and forgiveness.

Forgiveness restores a relationship that has been strained or broken. Through the blood of Jesus shed on the cross, Jesus paid the price for our sin and provided a means for us to receive God's gracious gift of forgiveness and experience a restored relationship with Him.

It's nothing we can do on our own.

Jesus took our punishment by taking our place. We should have been on that cross; we should have had to pay the price for our sin. He took our sin and exchanged it for righteousness; He took our severed, strained relationship with God and, in return, offers us healing, forgiveness, and restoration.

What a great deal! In one of his letters to the Corinthian church, Paul explains the completeness of what Christ did for us. *"Therefore, if anyone is in Christ, the new creation has come: The old has gone, the new is here! ...[21] God made him who had no sin to be sin for us, so that in him we might become the righteousness of God."* 2 Corinthians 5:17, 21

The Greek word for "in" is *"en"*, meaning a fixed position, with the primary idea of rest.[4]

For those who trust in Christ, our position in God's kingdom is secure. You can't be cut from the team or fired from the company. You don't have to worry about failing, disappointing God, or making mistakes. Once you are in Christ, you are a new creation. You have been given a new identity, and you are being remade, renewed, and restored.

Think of it this way: when you purchase books on Amazon, they give you a choice – you can buy the "brand-new-never-been-used-before" kind, or the "new to you" kind. These pre-owned, new-to-you books come with descriptions like "slightly damaged", "like new", or just plain "acceptable".

Dear friend, when you come to Christ you do not come as a "new-to-you" type of merchandise with all kinds of disclaimers and descriptions. In God's eyes, you are a brand-new, fresh-out-of-the-box, never-been-used-before creation!

Take a moment and let this sink in...what Jesus offers through the cross extends beyond forgiveness.

He came to make you whole.

He wants to empower you to live a new life. He desires to mold you into the kind of woman He originally had in mind for you to be when He created you.

Our response – out of gratitude for what Jesus has done – should be a desire to please Him and honor Him.

Now think about Simon and the woman who crashed his party in Luke 7. Both needed forgiveness, and both needed a blood sacrifice to pay the price for their sin. Both needed restoration. Both needed a new life. Both needed Jesus.

Who received it?

Luke doesn't tell us if Simon ever understood. The woman showed evidence of a changed life. She modeled a heart that desired Jesus and sought to please God.

For the woman, Jesus became a mirror by which she saw, possibly for the first time, the woman God had created her to be. She saw a clean slate, a fresh start, and a chance to start over.

How about you?

Have you received God's provision—the sacrifice of Jesus— for the forgiveness of your sins? Do you desire to live a life that honors God? Sometimes I think we're afraid to start because we don't know where to begin. It can be hard to find your way back when you've strayed so far off the path. It begins with repentance—making a U-turn. Turning away from sin and turning to God.

Would you like a chance to start over? If you haven't already done so, I invite you to receive God's forgiveness and a fresh start right now by praying this prayer:

"Dear Jesus, I want to know you. I want to live as you created and purposed for me to live. Today, I will stop trusting in myself, and start trusting in you and what your death accomplished for me when you died on the cross for my sin. You are holy, righteous and good, and I am a sinner. I repent for my sins and ask for your forgiveness. I invite you to come and live in my heart and be my Savior and my Lord. Make me the woman You created me to be. I commit myself to obeying You, every day, for the rest of my life. I love You."

It's been said that when Moravian missionaries took the message of God to the Eskimos, the missionaries struggled to find a word in the native language for forgiveness. They finally landed on this cumbersome twenty-four letter choice: *issumagijoujungnainermik*. This intimidating assembly of letters is translated as "not being able to think about it anymore."[5]

As someone who has trusted in Jesus, confessed their sin, and received God's forgiveness, you have a clean slate – a fresh start. While we may beat ourselves up over past sin and failures, God doesn't even think about it anymore.

He has removed the clouds of sin and shame. You can walk in the confidence and freedom that is yours in Christ and boldly approach Him, embracing all He has for you as His child.

5

You are Forgiving

Day 1 – Why Forgiveness Matters

For years, my son was mad at Pinocchio. (Yes, I'm referring to the fictional wooden puppet characterized in the classic children's novel and animated Disney movie.)

You couldn't even utter Pinocchio's name in our house without eliciting harsh words and opening tender wounds from Brandon. He was visibly hurt – deeply offended.

You're probably wondering, *"What heinous act could Pinocchio possibly have committed that produced SIX years of hurt and hostility in my child's heart?"*

During a trip to Disneyland when my son was three, Pinocchio took Brandon's beloved blankie. No, he didn't steal it. There was nothing malicious about it. Pinocchio simply admired it, borrowed it to cuddle with for a few seconds and gently returned it.

To Brandon, however, Pinocchio broke the cardinal toddler rule: *Never, ever, EVER touch the blankie of a three-year-old!* This was a direct infringement on his personal space and property. Brandon was persistent and determined NOT to let it go.

It was quite a family crisis. For years, we had many conversations which went as follows...

"Brandon, why won't you forgive Pinocchio?"

"He took my blankie."

"Pinocchio didn't take your blankie. He was just showing you how much he loved it."

"I don't like him, and I don't forgive him."

Finally, while on a trip to Disney World many years later, Brandon decided it was about time to end his six-year feud with the wooden puppet and extend forgiveness to Pinocchio. He'd let his anger stew long enough and needed to let it go.

With nervous determination, he entered the park.

Believe it or not, among the throngs of people at the Magic Kingdom, Pinocchio was the character chosen to greet eager Disney goers at the entrance that morning.

After waiting patiently in line to meet him, Brandon explained to Pinocchio how the blankie incident affected him, but he was now choosing to forgive him. Amends were made, and we enjoyed a wonderful day at the park.

Why is forgiveness hard sometimes? Why do we seem to find more pleasure in holding onto the offense than letting go of it?

When we choose to hold on to the offense, we're the ones who suffer – stomping around for days (perhaps years), clenching our jaw when a person's name is mentioned, hosting imaginary conversations, hoping for the chance to "tell them what we *really* think", secretly wanting them to fail – all as we wait for an apology that may never come.

It may satisfy us to hold onto the anger, nursing the grudge for a while. But unexpectedly, unforgiveness kills us, rotting us from the inside out like cancer, slowly draining life from our bodies.

Years ago, I remember an incident when a close friend deeply hurt me. As time passed, I thought I had forgiven her, but every time her name came up, I felt anger and frustration rise.

Whenever I talked about the incident to my husband, I would start tearing up. I had a hard time watching her succeed. (And to be completely honest, I secretly hoped she would retain her pregnancy weight. I know, that sounds so bad.) Clearly, I still had work to do on my heart.

The apostle Paul knew the danger unforgiveness had in a person's heart and a community. Aware of the danger of untended unforgiveness has in a heart, he warned the Ephesian church, "*Get rid of all bitterness, rage and anger, brawling and slander, along with every form of malice. [32] Be kind and compassionate to one*

another, forgiving each other, just as in Christ God forgave you."
Ephesians 4:31-32

Paul didn't talk about behavior modification. Instead, he instructed, get rid of your anger – all of it. Just like you get rid of your trash and get rid of the rotting food in your refrigerator, get rid of your bitterness, rage, and anger.

I'd like to think that by taking the trash out of my house once, I would never have to do it again. The reality is that I must continually do the work of removing spoiled food and smelly garbage from my home.

Daily.

Forgiveness requires us to bring our hurt before God, confront the pain in our heart, deal with our emotions and choose not to hold someone's past over them.

Today.

And again tomorrow.

And again, the next day.

As long as it takes until the weight is lifted.

Dear friend, this is the work of forgiveness. It's not a one and done prayer; it's a daily work of tending your heart. And when you do this work, you're able to breathe a little deeper, rest a little better and walk a whole lot lighter.

Forgive so you can be free again. Forgive so you can feel clean again. Forgive so you can have your life back.

Day Two – It Starts with a Choice

Many years ago, Gregg and I were having *aggressive negotiations* with each other (to borrow a term from *Star Wars*). More plainly stated, we were arguing. The intensity of the atmosphere was rising when our three-year-old daughter entered the room, pleading for our attention.

"Mom! Dad! What's this?"

Our efforts to encourage her patience paled in comparison to her persistence.

Unaware that she was interrupting a heated discussion, Becca proudly flashed her finger in the air to show us her intriguing discovery.

A big booger on her finger. Immediately the mood lightened as we burst into laughter and completely forgot about what had made us so angry just moments before.

While that momentary disagreement was easy to move past, it's not always that simple. When the wounds of offense cut deep, when an offense is repeated over and over, when trust is broken, and the relationship you once enjoyed is fractured and fragile, it's hard to forgive and move forward.

Much of the time, it's the people we love the most that hurt us the most. When we open our hearts to be vulnerable, we become intimately connected to them. It's risky to open our hearts to someone because it exposes us to potentially being hurt.

In Genesis 4:23-24, we learn about a man named Lamech. Lamech lived by the principle of revenge. He didn't get mad; he got even. He killed the person who had wronged him!

In dramatic contrast, when Jesus interacts with Peter years later, He alludes to this incident in Genesis, challenging Peter to respond differently to the people who hurt him.

"Then Peter came to Jesus and asked, 'Lord, how many times shall I forgive my brother or sister who sins against me? Up to seven times?' [22]Jesus answered, "I tell you, not seven times, but seventy-seven times." Matthew 18:21-22

In these verses, we find Peter asking Jesus the extent to which he needed to go to show forgiveness.

When would be enough? How many times must he set himself up to be hurt?

To be let down?

To be rejected?

Notice that the person who offended Peter was someone whom he considered *his brother*. Someone whom he had probably trusted, someone he loved, and someone who seemed to let Peter down time and time again.

Jesus alluded to Lamech's method of dealing with offense— the lifestyle of unforgiveness, anger, and revenge—and contrasted it with a completely different way to live.

A better way.

A way of life, not death; a way of forgiveness, not anger.

Jesus desires us to embrace a lifestyle of forgiveness that forgives so freely and liberally that it becomes a natural part of our life.

Where do we start? How do we take a step in this direction when it hurts so badly?

While it's one thing to know we should forgive, it's an entirely different thing to do it.

It starts with a choice.

We must choose to forgive. We must choose to take the path Jesus points us towards. A path that may be difficult, will most certainly be painful, and the journey could be a long one. But in the end, it's the path that will bring life and healing to our souls.

In choosing the way of Lamech, our souls become bitter and hard. Choosing the way of Jesus, while at times it doesn't make sense, allows His Spirit to work in our lives, eventually leading us to the freedom and wholeness we really desire.

Day Three – When I Don't Want to Forgive

Last summer, I received a frantic call from one of our college kids, *"Mom, how do I get rid of maggots?!"*

I'm grossed out even recalling the conversation.

Apparently, we had neglected to take out the trash in a timely manner. After an evening of fast-food trash mixed with the summer heat and humidity…well, you get the idea.

Let's return to Ephesians 4:31-32 and look at some of the ugly attitudes unforgiveness can breed if left unattended… *"Get rid of all bitterness, rage and anger, brawling and slander, along with every form of malice. ³² Be kind and compassionate to one another, forgiving each other, just as in Christ God forgave you."* Ephesians 4:31-32

Paul isn't a big fan of anger management. As we read a couple of days ago, his command to us is, *"Get rid of it!"* Just as you get rid of the trash and clutter in your home, get rid of the rubbish and mess in your heart. Don't let it harbor, fester, and grow uncontrolled.

Failure to do so will result in a heart filled with gross, creepy crawling things that seem to have a way of multiplying faster than you can get rid of them.

When someone hurts us, we can allow the wound to rage like wildfire in our hearts or snuff it out. Failure to smother our unforgiveness will scorch the relationship, and repeated cycles of not dealing with our offense can lead to an even greater problem – resentment.

When we become resentful, our hearts become hard. It's impossible to love and have compassion towards others to the degree God created us to do so if our hearts are hard and filled with gross maggoty things.

I realize it's counterintuitive to forgive when you've been hurt – especially when the pain is so debilitating. In these verses, Paul gives us two reasons why we should opt to make forgiveness a priority in our life.

We forgive others because Christ forgave us.

Jesus was rejected, humiliated, abandoned, betrayed, abused, and mocked, yet He chose forgiveness (Luke 23:34).

God chooses to extend forgiveness regardless of how we respond to Him. He's patient and continues to offer us an opportunity for relationship.

In fact, the prophet, Isaiah, relays a message from God to the Jewish people who had repeatedly offended, rejected, and betrayed God, *"I have swept away your offenses like a cloud, your sins like the morning mist. Return to me, for I have redeemed you."* Isaiah 44:22

Isn't that a beautiful illustration? God continually woos us, calling us to Himself. Every morning He chooses to wash our sins away like a morning mist that dissipates with just a little intensity from the sun.

The more we understand God's incredible and undeserved forgiveness toward us, the more we can extend this same forgiveness, mercy, and grace to others.

Think about it. God, who owns and created everything, sent His Son, Jesus, to suffer and be sacrificed for my sin while I was still hardheaded, stubborn, self-centered, and running away from God. Because of what Jesus did for you and me on the cross, we no longer have an excuse not to forgive. When we were unacceptable, God accepted us; when we were still in our sin, Christ died for us.

Our ability to extend forgiveness to others grows and expands as we understand and appreciate how much God has forgiven us. Instead of getting even and giving us what we deserved, He forgave us, taking away our sins by giving His life.

Out of gratitude, because of the greatness of our sin and the lavish provision of God to forgive us, we should model forgiveness to others.

Secondly, we forgive others because God asks us to forgive.

I love how Paul qualifies forgiveness for us – we are to forgive *just as Christ forgave you.* It's not something we should put off until we feel like dealing with it, nor is it a thing for which we wait to miraculously happen on its own.

We must choose to forgive, just as Christ forgave us.

When God asks us to forgive those who have hurt us, He asks us to do a very difficult but beautiful thing. He is asking us to come to a place in our heart where those who have wounded us, those who have wronged us, those who have taken advantage of us, or those who have brought us incredible pain don't owe us anything anymore.

Forgiveness can be a high-risk investment for many of us because when we choose to forgive, we give up the right to get even. God is asking us to set them free from whatever we have been holding against them.

To give up the right to get even.

To extend to them the fresh start that Jesus extended to us.

Maybe you feel someone robbed you of your childhood, job, reputation, marriage, time, or perhaps something else.

Forgiving doesn't validate what they did to you, but it cleans the junk out of your heart and sets you free to move forward.

Don't wait until you feel like it. I rarely feel like it.

When I've been hurt by someone, my natural tendency isn't to feel love and compassion toward them.

Instead, I find myself running imaginary conversations in my mind rehearsing what I *should've said* or *would've liked to say*. It's embarrassing to admit, but if I'm honest, I'm not hoping for the best for them. My "prayers" for them consist of things like praying that their car will break down or their toilets will overflow.

I must remember (or sometimes my husband has to remind me) to choose a different path.

Dear friend, this is the hard work of forgiveness – the daily job of choosing to let go of offense. To daily clean your heart.

The future quality of your life doesn't depend on your past, as much as it is determined by how you respond to what you have experienced, and how you move forward. At some point, you have to choose.

Forgiving someone won't change the past— but it can change your future.

God has an amazing future for you. While you can't change your past, nor can you control how people treat you, you can control the kind of person you become.

Day Four – Do We Have to Be Friends?

One of the questions often raised about forgiveness is, *"Does this mean I have to be friends with the person who hurt me?"*

In a perfect world, yes…but this world isn't perfect – it's broken and sinful. And as Taylor Swift so eloquently stated, *all some people ever gonna be is mean.*[1]

With that said, when you find yourself in a relationship with someone who uses their words as weapons to tear you down, their attitudes to demean you, or their actions are intent on dragging you down, it's your responsibility to create healthy boundaries in the relationship. Which means there are times when you will do the heart-work required to forgive, but you'll still have to create space in the relationship.

Forgiveness isn't synonymous with reconciliation. God commands us to forgive those who hurt us, but He doesn't require reconciliation. While I believe God's heart is for unity and reconciliation should be the long-term goal and desire, sometimes it's just not that easy.

In Psalm 147, the psalmist describes the heart of God towards His children, *"He heals the brokenhearted and binds up their wounds."* Psalm 147:3

Webster's dictionary defines "broken" as being violently separated into parts, shattered, damaged, or altered. This definition depicts *brokenheartedness* as being overcome by grief or despair. Doesn't that accurately describe how we feel when someone hurts or betrays us?

The pain can be intense and overwhelming. And in instances where the offense is particularly traumatic, even thinking about the person who hurt us can be paralyzing. The distance between them and us feels like a vast ocean that is impossible to cross.

God is such a loving, healing God. In this verse, the psalmist describes God as a caring Father who *binds up* the brokenhearted. The Hebrew word for *bind up* is *châbash*, which means to tie or bandage.

When my children get injured, the first thing they want is a Band-Aid. Firmly wrapping their wound gives them comfort. It also helps the wound to stay clean of infection so it can heal properly.

Your life may consist of a string of painful experiences where relationships have been shattered by betrayal, rejection, and sin. Jesus came to clean your wounds of hurt, anger, and bitterness. He came to "bind them up", to heal, restore, and make you whole, so you can live the full life that He created you to live.

A major step in receiving all God has for you begins with forgiving those who have hurt you. But forgiveness doesn't always include reconciliation.

Forgiving someone is something you choose to do, whether the other person desires it or not. Forgiveness doesn't require you to work things through with the person who offended you. I hope that happens, but that's reconciliation, not forgiveness.

Reconciliation requires the cooperation of the other person to make it happen. Sometimes reconciliation takes years, and sometimes it never happens. If you make reconciliation the condition you require before you're willing to forgive them, you'll hold yourself hostage to the person who hurt you.

Possibly, you've been deeply hurt, violated, betrayed. Maybe someone gossiped about you, lied about you, took advantage of you, or perhaps your spouse cheated, your parent abandoned you, or someone hurt someone you love.

Our most painful hurt often comes from those we love and trust the most. Because we open our hearts and make ourselves vulnerable, the pain is even more intense.

I don't want to, in any way, minimize or trivialize your hurt, but I do know that if you carry hurt and unforgiveness, it will poison your soul. It will spread to those around you and destroy your relationships with others and God.

You are Forgiving

Here's my prayer for you. Allow God to gently resurface and reveal the work of forgiveness you still need to do.

Maybe your business partner didn't deliver, or your close friend betrayed your trust, or your mom or dad did something to hurt you. Perhaps your teenage child rejected you, or your spouse broke trust. Or maybe your offense is with someone who's no longer living or possibly you were so young you can't remember who it is that hurt you. Maybe you're angry with God because He could have done something and He didn't and you're thinking, *"Why didn't you?!"*

Take a step and forgive. You may never be friends with them, but you don't have to make that your goal. Your goal is to clean out the gunk in your heart so you can move forward in what God has for you.

What is impossible with man is possible with God. I'm praying that by the power of the Holy Spirit, God will give you His grace and power to forgive.

Day Five – Walking in Forgiveness

In the Old Testament, we're introduced to a man named Joseph, who modeled a lifestyle of forgiveness. Perhaps you've heard of him – fancy coat, thrown in a pit, unjustly sent to prison. Yeah, that guy.

95

Joseph's eleven older brothers, fed up with his boasting and the favoritism shown towards him by their father, plotted to kill him (Genesis 37:12-28). At the last minute, they changed their plans and chose to humiliate Joseph, strip him and throw him into a dark hole, and sell him as a slave to Egypt (how kind of them).

Once he arrived in Egypt, things went from bad to worse. Joseph was falsely accused of a crime, thrown in prison, and forgotten for years.

You may know someone so weighed down with hurt and anger they no longer trust anyone. Joseph was a man who had every reason to live full of mistrust, anger, bitterness, and revenge. Instead, he chose a different path.

Scripture shows us how Joseph worked to keep bitterness and anger from holding a place in his heart. The little indication we see of Joseph even acknowledging his hardship and suffering is found in the names he chose for his sons (Genesis 41:51-52).

Joseph could have rightly had a lot of issues with a lot of people. He didn't deny his hardships but determined not to allow his past suffering to hinder his present effectiveness for God.

When Joseph is finally reunited with his brothers many years later, he recalls the incident with his brothers that inevitably led to his years of dark loneliness.

"But don't be upset, and don't be angry with yourselves for selling me to this place. It was God who sent me here ahead of you to preserve your lives." Genesis 45:5 NLT

The people who hurt us won't always come and bow before us, begging for mercy, as in Joseph's case. You may never receive the kind of closure and restoration that Joseph received, but we can apply some powerful principles from Joseph's example to help keep our hearts clean from the pain of hurt and unforgiveness. How did he do it?

1. Recognize God's sovereign plan for your life.

God had a special plan for Joseph's life, and He has a special plan for your life. Through all the challenges, offense, and strained relationships, God was with Joseph, working something special in his life.

You may wonder why you had to go through what you did; you may wonder where God was during your painful season. And you may never have all the answers.

So often, my focus can drift to mantras of "Why me?...", "If only...," and "It's not fair!..." I momentarily forget that, like Joseph, God has a plan for my life, and my purpose is to know Him and I may not always know or understand His plan!

My friend, God promises to be with you, to guide you, to comfort you, and to build His character and likeness inside of you as you choose to forgive, as you choose to keep your heart clean of unforgiveness.

2. Acknowledge with whom you're angry and why you're hurt.

Identifying the people with whom we are angry and bitter is usually easy. It is more difficult to determine why we're so hurt. What did they do to you?

Did they steal your job, consume years of your time, ruin your marriage, deprive you of the opportunity to grow up in a loving home, or is it something more intangible? For you to move forward, it is necessary to do the difficult work of discovering what you feel was wrongfully taken from your life.

I remember investing years into a friendship that left me feeling abandoned and betrayed. It wasn't until I realized the source of my hurt that I was finally able to move forward and experience freedom, healing, and forgiveness.

Forgiving someone doesn't mean you agree with what they did, nor does it make them right. It frees you from bearing the weight of hurt and bitterness, and empowers God to heal you and help you move on.

3. Experience God's grace.

The ability to forgive someone who inflicted such pain in your life is only possible by the power of God's Spirit living inside of you. The presence of His Spirit in your life will empower you to do anything God asks of you—even if it seems impossible. He is with you; He is on your side.

As you trust in God's grace and allow His power to work through your weakness, you will be amazed at what you can accomplish.

As you choose to forgive, healing will begin in your heart. It begins with a choice to forgive – and to keep forgiving. At first, it may be hard, painful, and cut against the grain of what you feel like doing.

Shauna Neiquist likens this feeling to "moving a piano all the way across the living room, and then waking up the next morning and finding that it's back in the other corner, and you must move it again. Every day you have to push that heavy piano all the way across the living room, even though you just did it the day before.[2]

Eventually, the piano will be easier to move, and one day you'll find that you don't have to move it at all!

4. Keep moving forward!

The future quality of your life doesn't depend on your past, as much as it is determined by how you respond to what you have experienced and how you choose to move forward. At some point, you must choose to move on.

Hosting a continuous pity party and holding on to past hurts never helps (although it sure feels good!). Sometimes the people with whom you are angry often are not even burdened with guilt by their actions. Occasionally, they're entirely unaware they have hurt you!

I've said it before, but it's worth repeating: you can't change your past, nor can you control how people treat you. However, you can control the kind of person you become.

Don't hold on to anger and bitterness. Jesus offers you a new way to live.

He forgave you, and now He asks you to forgive others so someday you can stand before God with a clean heart, having fulfilled His whole purpose for your life.

6

You are Loved

Day One – A True Love Story

Let me share a love story with you. Not a love story scripted by Disney or cast by Hollywood, but one written long ago by God through an Old Testament prophet named Hosea.

Hosea lived during the 8th century BC – a dark and tumultuous time in Israel's history. Six different kings reigned in Israel during a brief period of 25 years - four of whom were brutally assassinated by their successors during their reign. Not an environment for building national morale or breeding peace and security.

It was a despairing period in the history of Israel, not only because Israel lacked consistent godly leadership but also because the Jewish people had once again strayed from intimately walking with God.

Yet God, in His mercy, did the same thing He had always done—the same thing He still does today. He lovingly sought out His lost children by working through a young prophet who demonstrated God's undying love for His people.

God spoke to Hosea and instructed him to marry a woman. But here's where the story gets a little weird – and awkward.

While we would expect God to encourage Hosea to marry a godly woman who faithfully serves alongside him, God tells him to marry a prostitute. Seriously! God continues to explain that even some of the children born during their marriage will be children from his wife's promiscuity (Hosea 1:1-3). What?!

You may be asking, *"Why on earth would God ask someone (especially a prophet) to marry someone like that?"*

Someone they couldn't trust.

Someone who would most assuredly break their heart into a thousand pieces – not just once, but many times.

Through Hosea, God was illustrating that although Israel has repeatedly been unfaithful and disloyal in their relationship with God, He remains faithful because of His immense love for them. Their infidelity didn't diminish God's love for them or His faithfulness to them.

Hosea married Gomer and loved her with the same love, compassion, and care God extends to all His children, even the wayward and unfaithful ones.

Despite having a loving husband, and all her needs provided, Gomer still chose to wander from the security and safety of her home, continuing her lifestyle of promiscuity and unfaithfulness.

Gomer gave birth to three children, but it's questionable whether Hosea was the father of two of them (remember, this is before DNA testing).

Hosea's pain for his family and the nation of Israel is revealed by the names he chose for his children. Aware of God's impending judgment on Israel, Hosea named his oldest son, *Jezreel*, meaning *God Scatters*.

When Gomer became pregnant with her second child, a daughter, Hosea named her *Lo Ruhamah*, meaning *Not Loved*. How heartbreaking! Her name represented a reversal of the love and compassion that God had once had for Israel. God, who had been longsuffering and merciful to His children, was now saying He would withhold His love and mercy and bring judgment on His wayward children.

And just when you think the story couldn't get any worse or more tragic...

Gomer gives birth to another son named *Lo Ammi*, meaning *Not My People*. God has decided their wickedness is too great, and He must break His covenant with them.

This same God who had been intimately involved with them for centuries... This same God who delivered them from slavery in Egypt... This same God who had parted the Red Sea and provided them with manna for forty years in the wilderness... This same God whose presence had led them by a cloud during the day and a pillar of fire by night... This same God who delivered them from their enemies and promised to be with them, walking alongside them, caring for and providing for them.

This same God says, they will no longer be considered *His people,* and He will no longer call Himself *their God.*

Gomer's determination to flee from and reject any type of pure love, affection, and affirmation of worth, eventually led to her running away to pursue other lovers. She left everything of value and worth in her life—her husband, her children, and her home— to seek empty, immediate pleasure.

How humiliating for Hosea! Imagine the shame. Think of the rampant gossip at the expense of his family. After all, he was a prophet in Israel!

Gomer not only dishonored his name with her promiscuity and rude behavior, but she also took for granted everything with which he had blessed her. She even refused to acknowledge Hosea as the true source of everything she enjoyed by carelessly squandering his wealth and giving her lovers credit for things he had given her.

Yet as hurt, angry and betrayed as Hosea must have felt, he never stopped pursuing her. He sought after Gomer, searching diligently for her, and upon finding her, discovered she had become enslaved to one of her lovers.

Hosea bought her back, paying the price of a slave for her, but he didn't treat her with anything less than the love, honor, and respect deserving of a wife. He didn't shame her; he brought her home, cleaned her up, and restored the blessing, affirmation, and love of a family.

In fact, not only was Gomer restored, but everything belonging to her was restored as well. Her children were given new names: *My People* and *My Loved One*. Hosea's patience, love, compassion, and grace redeemed Gomer's past and brought forth future blessings for her and for his family.[1]

God speaks through Hosea, *"I will plant her for myself in the land; I will show my love to the one I called 'Not my loved one.' I will say to those called 'Not my people,' 'You are my people'; and they will say, 'You are my God.'"* Hosea 2:23

The experience of Hosea and Gomer provides just a tiny glimpse into God's unconditional love for you and the great extent He will go to bring His lost children home.

Our human experience is limited, and we often struggle to understand and comprehend the depths of God's love. God continues, despite our mistakes, to relentlessly pursue us and demonstrate His immense love toward us again and again.

During one of Israel's darkest hours, God shone a bright light of grace and redemption. God provided an opportunity for complete restoration.

An invitation for His lost daughter to come home.

Day Two – This is True Love

Years ago, Gregg gave me a card for my birthday that on the cover read: *I love you more today than yesterday.* On the inside, it continued: *Yesterday, you really got on my nerves.*

Gregg assured me it was just a joke, and we had a good laugh. But isn't that how many people view God's love for them – changing, fluctuating, circumstantial?

Even though I know *in my head* God's love towards me is constant and unchanging, sometimes *my heart* wavers and falls short of truly believing it and living like it.

When we have relationships where love is conditional, our natural response is fear and insecurity. One wrong step, and we may lose the relationship.

We work harder to earn love and prove we're worthy of it. We put up walls to protect ourselves from being hurt. We keep those we care about at a distance because we fear they would no longer love us if they really knew us. We control our circumstances and make calculated decisions that minimize risk to the relationship.

And we follow a similar pattern in our attempt to have a relationship with God.

But this isn't how God describes love at all!

God's love is an outpouring of His kindness and goodness toward His creation. It's not a love you have earned or even deserve.

He is the pursuer; He is the romancer; He is the One initiating a relationship with you. He loves you simply because He created you. You can do absolutely nothing to earn or deserve it. And equally important, there is absolutely nothing that would cause Him to withhold His love for you.

Let's look at how the apostle, John, describes God's kind of love in scripture. *"Dear friends, let us love one another, for love comes from God. Everyone who loves has been born of God and knows God.⁸ Whoever does not love does not know God, because God is love."* 1 John 4:7-8

God is love! Love is the core of His being and the essence of His nature. God cannot possibly act in any way contrary to His divine nature.

In all that He is and in all that He does, God is love. Love is the motivation and driving force behind everything He is and does.

Let's explore this idea one step further and look at *love* as described by the apostle Paul in 1 Corinthians 13:4-8, *"Love is patient, love is kind. It does not envy, it does not boast, it is not proud. ⁵ It does not dishonor others, it is not self-seeking, it is not easily angered, it keeps no record of wrongs. [6] Love does not delight in evil but rejoices with the truth. [7] It always protects, always trusts, always hopes, always perseveres. [8] Love never fails."* 1 Corinthians 13:4-8a

Stay with me a minute, and let's put two and two together.

If God is love, and love is described in the verses above by these many noble attributes, then wouldn't it be accurate to say that God is also all those things?

Let's reread these verses and insert *God* for *love*:

God is patient, God is kind. God does not envy or boast, He is not proud... God does not delight in evil, but rejoices with the truth. God always protects, always trusts, always hopes, and always perseveres. God never fails.

Sometimes when we experience challenges and pain in our life, it can distort how we see God.

Maybe your father has a volatile temper, so you naturally think God will be angry when you make mistakes.

Maybe your parents divorced, so you struggle to believe God will be there when you need Him.

Maybe your family tends to be harsh and keeps a record of offenses, so you feel God cannot forgive you from your past.

Maybe your friends have let you down and you can't see God as always being faithful.

Regardless of what your past perception has been concerning God as your Heavenly Father, He is loving, patient, kind, humble, gentle, faithful, and totally good in who He is and all He does.

Knowing that the Lord of the universe loves you is the strongest foundation that any human can have. A growing awareness of God's love in Christ is the greatest reward.[2]

Once we begin to understand this more clearly and believe it more fully, the natural result will be trust and security in God that anchors our life and our relationship with God and others.

What a beautiful gift we can share with others.

Day Three – To Infinity and Beyond!

Love is a word that's used extensively to describe many different things. Here are just a few from my recent vocabulary…

I love coffee. I love dark chocolate. I love puppies. I love fresh mangoes. I love a day at the beach. I love avocados. I love surfing. I love USC football… (Fight On!)

The problem in using the word "love" to describe the created things we enjoy is we inadvertently diminish the potency of God's incredible love for us.

Our English word, *love*, is far too limiting to describe the kind of love God has demonstrated toward us. The Greek language has four words describing *love* and how it's expressed.

Agape is the Greek word used to describe the love God demonstrates toward us. It's an affectionate, benevolent love. It's the highest, most noble kind of love, and it's used throughout the New Testament to describe God's love for people and the kind of love we should have for God.

John, one of Jesus' closest friends, explains, *"God showed how much he loved us by sending his one and only Son into the world so that we might have eternal life through him.*[10] *This is real love—not that we loved God, but that he loved us and sent his Son as a sacrifice to take away our sins."* 1 John 4:9-10

You may not feel it, you may not believe it, but God loves you. He loves you so passionately and extravagantly that while you were still running away from Him, He sacrificed His only Son so you could experience the fullness and richness of His love.

If you're a parent, you get this. You willingly make sacrifices for your kids because you love them. You're not looking for what they can give back to you. You love them simply because they're your children.

God's love, demonstrated to us through the death of Jesus, was completely unconditional and totally undeserved. There were no expectations to be met or exemptions to be had, no demands for our perfection and obedience, no disclaimers regarding our faults. The love God extends to us literally has no strings attached.

He loves us, not because of what we offer Him or give back to Him. He loves us because He created us. We're His children.

J. I. Packer, in his book, *Knowing God*, defines God's love as an "exercise of His goodness towards individual sinners whereby, having identified himself with their welfare, he has given his Son to be their Savior, and now brings them to know and enjoy him in covenant relationship."[3]

God doesn't choose to love some of His children while simultaneously refusing to love others. He doesn't love His children when they obey Him and then withhold His love when they don't.

God's love has no limits. His love always protects, always trusts, always hopes, and always perseveres. God's capacity to love is never maxed out. God's love never says, *"You've crossed the line and gone too far. I can't love you now."*

He knows your hidden secrets and your inner longings. All your quirks, flaws, and crummy attitudes. Still, He loves you with an immense, everlasting love that is steadfast and unchanging.

The Old Testament prophet, Jeremiah, reminds the wayward people of Israel, *"Long ago the Lord said to Israel: "I have loved you, my people, with an everlasting love. With unfailing love I have drawn you to myself."* Jeremiah 31:3

The Hebrew word for everlasting in this verse is *ôlâm* which means forever, eternal, perpetual, and to the vanishing point. Or, as Buzz Lightyear would say, "To infinity and beyond!"

I used to approach my relationships thinking if people saw all my flaws and areas of weakness, they wouldn't like me anymore. But you can't have a real relationship that's not real!

True love, the kind of love God has for us and desires us to display to a broken world, is a love that will love us despite our flaws and failings. Despite all our quirks and idiosyncrasies.

If you're afraid to be yourself and hiding who you truly are, your relationships will be shallow and inauthentic, won't they? You'll also be exhausted, too!

Trust me, it's a lot of work to wear a mask. But it's freeing to be yourself—the whole goofy package—and yet still know and be assured that in Christ you loved with an everlasting love that has no bounds.

Day Four – A Love that Never Gives Up

Several years ago, to check something off my bucket list, I trained for and ran a marathon. One of the key training points they coach and prepare you for is the inevitable *"hitting the wall"*.

In distance competitions, *hitting the wall* is a sensation in your body when you experience a dramatic depletion of energy. Your training is intended to prepare you mentally and physically to endure the pain, to push through this intense desire to give up so you can finish the race.

Through the first half of the race, I felt strong, kept my pace, and prepared for the final stretch – the long, gradual 2.5-mile incline up what had been dubbed *Heartbreak Hill*.

Around mile 23, my body began to shut down. My legs felt like lead poles I had to lug every step. Everything in me wanted to give up and go home.

But I didn't. I dragged my body to the finish line because I knew the pain was temporary, and the joy I would experience in less than an hour would be worth it if I didn't give up.

I endured the pain in hopes of experiencing something greater.

My friend, Jesus' love for you is an enduring love. Look at how the writer of Hebrews describes the determination of Jesus and what He endured for you and me. *"For the joy set before him he endured the cross, scorning its shame, and sat down at the right hand of the throne of God. ³ Consider him who endured such opposition from sinners, so that you will not grow weary and lose heart."* Hebrews 12:2b-3

Twice, in just two verses, the writer uses the word, *endured*, to describe what Jesus went through on the cross.

What He endured for *you*.

The Greek word is *hupomeno,* which means to stay under, to remain, to bear (trials), have fortitude, persevere.[4]

If you are ever tempted to doubt God's love for you, consider the pain and suffering Jesus endured to pay the price to provide a way for you to be restored to relationship with God. Think about the shame and suffering He experienced; reflect on the betrayal and the loneliness He willingly subjected Himself to.

He didn't run away from the cross. He didn't give up. He endured. Because of the joy before Him. The joy of fulfilling the Father's will and experiencing eternity with you. All because of His enduring love for His heavenly Father and for *you*.

Perhaps you have a friendship that failed to weather the storm of a disagreement. Maybe your marriage didn't make it, or your parent's marriage didn't make it.

When we experience the hurt and pain that human relationships can bring, it can lead us to believe that God will do the same to us.

God's love isn't like that. God won't leave you; He won't forsake you. Even the best of human relationships will fall short compared to the enduring love a relationship with God offers. You can count on God's love toward you to endure forever.

Here's even better news! Not only will God not give up on you (sorry, I threw a double negative in there); He won't allow anything to stand in the way of His love and you. His love for you isn't strained, straggling across the finish line into eternity. It's a love that is secure, unwavering, and unchanging.

In his attempt to communicate the steadfast love of Christ, Paul writes to the Roman church assuring them, *"Who shall separate us from the love of Christ? Shall trouble or hardship or persecution or famine or nakedness or danger or sword? ...For I am convinced that neither death nor life, neither angels nor demons, neither the present nor the future, nor any powers, [39] neither height nor depth, nor anything else in all creation, will be able to separate us from the love of God that is in Christ Jesus our Lord."* Romans 8:35, 38-39

Nothing can separate you from God's love. Nothing is beyond the reach of His loving arm. Nothing can cause Him to turn away from you in disgrace or lead Him to refuse to lovingly embrace you as His child.

Remember how God's love is derived from the Greek word *agape*? Vine's Expository Dictionary defines *agape*: "[Agape love] expresses the deep and constant love and interest of a perfect being towards entirely unworthy subjects."[5]

Maybe your life currently reflects a disinterest in God; He is crazy about you. Perhaps you don't yet possess a deep passion for Him; He is madly in love with you.

Our children are growing older, and we are now a home of teenagers and young adults. Gone are the days when they crawl into our bed at night and express how much they love us. They prefer I not hug them in front of their friends or even post pictures of them on Instagram without their permission. In fact, there have even been a couple of days when their attitudes and actions would lead me to question their love for me.

Yet, even on the most difficult of days, my love for them has never wavered or diminished. Not. Even. An. Inch.

When God sees us wandering away from Him, I think He feels the same way about us. Because of His immense love for us, He won't push us away. He's longing for us to reach out to Him, to look for Him, to trust Him, and to come home.

It's hard to fathom that a perfect God, who is holy and blameless, would express such an unconditional, faithful, and enduring love towards us – His uninterested, unloving, and selfish children. Yet, that's what He does. And that's what He'll continue to do. Because He thinks you're worth it.

Day Five – Because of Love

One of the most familiar Bible verses is John 3:16. You don't have to be a theologian to know it – just watch any football game, and you're likely to see a banner waving it in one of the end zones. Let's jump right in and read it.

"For God so loved the world that he gave his one and only Son, that whoever believes in him shall not perish but have eternal life." John 3:16

God didn't just love the world; He *so* loved it.

Years ago, we had a beloved pet rabbit named Angel. My children would express their love for Angel saying, *"We love her so, so, so much!"*

"So." It's a little adverb that packs a big punch.

"So." To such a great extent.

Dear friend, that's how God feels about you. He loves you so, so, so much. In this verse, it wasn't enough for Jesus to tell Nicodemus God loved the world. He made sure to emphasize the magnitude of God's love.

God couldn't bear the thought of being separated from you. God's love for you was the motivation behind His glorious plan of redemption. His love is a lavish, extravagant love that is heaped upon you without any limitations or expectations.

Take a moment to ponder the extravagance of God's love, as written by Hannah Whitall Smith:

"Put together all the tenderest love you know of, the deepest you have ever felt and the strongest that has ever been poured out on you, and heap upon it all the love of all the loving human hearts in the world and then multiply it by infinity and you will begin, perhaps, to have some faint glimpse of what the love of God is."[6]

Over the last few days, we've set our hearts to catch a glimpse of God's amazing love for us. It's a love that pales in comparison to anything we've claimed to love or anyone we've deeply loved.

We've learned God is love—it is the *essence* of who He is. We've also discovered His love is *everlasting* and *enduring*.

How should we respond to this amazing love, undeservedly lavished on us by a gracious God?

He asks only one thing from us.

Extend this love to others.

With the birth of each of my children, God has enlarged my heart to instantly love my new child with immeasurable love. I didn't have to learn to love my new child, nor did I have to take some love away from my other children to make room in my heart to love them.

God has made us to be like Him in this incredible way: He has given us a limitless capacity to love others with extravagant love. In Christ, there is no limit to our capacity to love. A desire to demonstrate this love to others should naturally flow from our gratitude for the love God showed to us.

Granted, our sinful hearts and selfish desires often inhibit us from stepping out of our comfort zone into the hurting world around us. Yet, this is how He created us to live—to take the extravagant, abundant, enduring, everlasting love God has shown towards us and extend it to others.

God desires for us to model Christ's love to the world. When we do, not only do they encounter Christ, but we flourish as well. We flourish because this is how God created us to live—with our life poured out for others.

It's not about keeping a bunch of rules and doing the right things; it's living with our life extended outward with an enlarged capacity to love and serve His children in a broken world.

Knowing and believing God's love for you should influence how you live. God's love is real, and as you believe and embrace it, you will begin to see dramatic changes in your life.

Remember Hosea? Hosea's love for God, his wife, and the wayward nation of Israel motivated him not to stop loving – regardless of if they reciprocated the love. He refused to allow insecurity, self-pity, selfishness, and bitterness to fester in his heart.

Our love for God and His children should motivate us to set aside our needs and desires to love and serve those around us in hopes that they, too, would come to know and experience the incredible love of Jesus.

In 1 John 3:16-18, Jesus' closest friend, John, talks about God's love and the outcome it should produce in our lives, *"This is how we know what love is: Jesus Christ laid down his life for us. And we ought to lay down our lives for our brothers and sisters. [17] If anyone has material possessions and sees a brother or sister in need but has no pity on them, how can the love of God be in that person? [18] Dear children, let us not love with words or speech but with actions and in truth."* 1 John 3:16-18

Every person you see, every person with whom you interact at work, at your child's school, on the soccer field, at the grocery store, on the freeway (Lord, help us) . . . is someone so deeply and extravagantly loved by God that He sent his Son to die for them.

Imagine what your life—your marriage, your family, and your community—would look like if this became the lens through which you viewed all your interactions with others? How could this change even your most routine and mundane tasks?

As for me, this reminder challenges me to slow down. To not fill my schedule with so much activity that I'm unable to pause, enjoy and love people. How about you?

A woman who truly loves God and is convinced and secure in God's love for her will demonstrate this love through generously serving others. She won't interpret the needs of others as an inconvenience or a burden but as opportunities to express the true essence of God's nature: the everlasting, enduring, and extravagant love of a Father.

7

You are Valuable

Day One – Work of Art

Antiques Roadshow is a reality show on PBS where people bring items they've acquired and present them to knowledgeable antique dealers who appraise the article's value. Over the years, they've made some surprising discoveries.

Several years ago, the show featured two antique dealers admiring a simple and somewhat plain card table. The owner described her table as a "moldy mess" but added she liked its style. She had purchased it at a yard sale for $25 after talking the owner down from $30.

Believe it or not, this insignificant-looking piece of furniture turned out to be an extremely valuable table that caught the eye of the show's hosts. In an inconspicuous part of the table, they noticed a faded label that could still be read, *"John Seymour and Sons of Boston"*. This table that appeared plain was crafted by a furniture maker from the 1800s who made high-end furniture for some of Boston's wealthiest people.

While someone like myself would have dismissed it as an old card table that had seen better days, this was a rare mahogany table with delicate satinwood inlay. Once restored, the true beauty of the table was revealed, and this simple, unassuming table was appraised at $250,000! It gets even better. Upon going to auction at Sotheby's, the piece fetched $541,500![1]

(Perhaps we should pause and go rummage through our attics or garages for some valuable stuff we've overlooked.)

A friend of mine has quite a bit of knowledge about antiques. She will visit garage sales and sometimes find incredible things bearing price tags much less than their true worth. She once told me you often find articles of great value being sold at unbelievably low prices because people don't know the value of what they have.

Often, the item has been neglected or poorly cared for because the owner failed to recognize the worth of their stuff.

Do you see where this is headed?

Sadly, many women see themselves like that old card table—broken, damaged, insignificant, and not worth much. As a result, they treat themselves and think about themselves in a like manner.

They destroy their bodies through food or drug addictions, give themselves to unhealthy relationships, do anything to be accepted by their peers, and neglect to take care of themselves.

My friend, God wants you to know and truly believe your worth and value. You have worth because God – the creator of the universe and the author of life – created you and gave you the gift of life. He wants to restore your brokenness so your true beauty can shine through.

Let's return to this scripture in Ephesians. It's one of my faves. *"For we are God's masterpiece. He has created us anew in Christ Jesus, so we can do the good things he planned for us long ago."* Ephesians 2:10 NLT

You are a masterpiece, created and loved by God.

Michelangelo's *Pietà* is considered by many as one of the greatest sculptures of Renaissance art. The *Pietà* is a large marble sculpture of the Virgin Mary holding the crucified body of Christ.

Years ago, someone attacked the statue and began smashing it with a sledgehammer. Although significant damage was done, Vatican artists worked carefully and meticulously and were able to restore the statue to near-perfect condition.[2]

God is at work in your life to restore what has been defaced and destroyed. Like layers of dust on a piece of furniture, our hearts collect residue of hurt, betrayal, offense, insecurity, and rejection over the years.

As you allow God to do a little restoration in your life, He will begin to buffer out the dings, strip away the gunk, and polish up the dull finish, so the true beauty of Christ can shine through.

Then you can partner with God in the "good things" He has for you! These "things" aren't "to-do" lists; they're not lists of achievements or a ladder to success. And they won't gain you greater love or acceptance from God.

The *good things* God has for you are things He has uniquely created for you to do; it's your life purpose and calling. He knows who He created you to be and when you're in His purpose, you're truly living and flourishing.

It starts with knowing the true value of who you are in Christ because you are His work of art.

Day Two – Wonderfully Made

In our home, we have an item I consider very valuable, rare, and unique. It's one-of-kind, yet I went 18 years without even seeing it. Until recently, my kids had never seen it. I used it only once and then carefully packed it into a box where it remains to this day. It didn't cost much money, yet it's invaluable and irreplaceable to me—even though I'll probably never use it again.

It's my wedding dress.

During one of our cross-country moves, Gregg suggested I give it away. (That didn't go over very well.) I pleaded my case and stated my defense, and the dress was saved.

It's natural for us to treat valuable possessions differently than we treat items of lesser worth. We care for them; we guard and protect them. Sometimes we even insure them or lock them away in a safe deposit box.

But often, over time and with repeated use, we begin to invest less care and pay less attention to these valuables.

The new car we meticulously washed and vacuumed eventually acquires a few scratches and dings. The latest version of our iPhone we cared for and cradled, cracks. Or our new favorite super-cute shirt we wore only on the most special occasions, picks up a stain.

When something of value begins to lose its shiny "newness", we move on. We look for a different car, purchase the even-newer-latest-and-greatest iPhone, and shop for the *Instyle* magazine fashion-forward clothing items.

Thankfully, God isn't like this.

He doesn't discard us when we get wrinkles, lose our "thigh gap", or surrender to the battle of gray hair.

My son, Jordan, has a stuffed penguin named Mumble who's been in our family since Jordan was five. When Jordan was little, Mumble was elevated to the status of a family pet. He accompanied us on family vacations and even made an occasional trip to school in my son's backpack.

Even though Jordan is older now and doesn't play with Mumble anymore, we all still love this little penguin and wouldn't think of getting rid of it. As dirty and tattered as Mumble has become (especially now that our dog loves to play with it), we would never think of trading Mumble for a cleaner, newer model. Mumble has value for our family, even with all his wear and tear.

Your life has extreme value to God. You are one-of-a-kind to Him, even in your sinful, tattered, aging, less-fit shape, there is no one else just like you. And He thinks you're awesome!

In Psalm 139, David describes it this way, *"For you created my inmost being; you knit me together in my mother's womb. [14] I praise you because I am fearfully and wonderfully made; your works are wonderful, I know that full well."* Psalm 139:13-14

This psalm is one of those passages of scripture you'll want to highlight in your Bible, write on an index card to post on your bathroom mirror to meditate on whenever you begin to doubt your unique worth and value.

David declares that *he is fearfully and wonderfully made...* It's sometimes easier to acknowledge the wonder of God in other people than to admit it about ourselves.

You belong to God. He has created you to share an intimate relationship with Him. God didn't create you to merely exist. He created you with purpose, on purpose, for a purpose.

You are Valuable

You are valuable to God simply because He created you. He formed you in your mother's womb, and He loves you. You were not an accident nor a surprise to God. Even if your natural parents didn't "plan" your birth or "want" you, God did. Before the foundation of the world, He knew you and planned your life to hold a specific and unique place in His Kingdom.

Nothing can fulfill you as Jesus can—not your position at work, your degree, your husband, your boyfriend, your achievements, your children, your friends, or your parents. None is a valid source to affirm your worth and value.

Sometimes knowing people need us, look to us and make us feel good can become substitutes for the real thing. We depend on their approval to prop us up, but when the affirmation ceases, the ache in our hearts for value screams even louder.

Regardless of what others have said about your value, worth, or usefulness, God sees you as valuable in His sight; He purchased you with the blood of His very own Son, and He doesn't make poor investments.

My friend, God created you to be you, and He thinks you're a masterpiece, carefully and artfully, *wonderfully made*.

Day Three – Fancy Hats

I purchased a fascinator today. You know those tiny hats that don't fit over your entire head? Yup, one of those. To be clear, these aren't a part of my daily wardrobe. I'm more of a trucker-hat-kinda-girl. But in a rush of spontaneity and an upcoming women's event, I paid the $7 and clicked "buy now". Because you never know when an invitation to dinner with the King (or with Kate or Meaghan, for that matter) will arrive. I'm still waiting. But you gotta be prepared for these kinds of emergencies.

Anyway, this got me thinking about how enamored our culture is with royalty.

Exactly how many Disney princesses are there now?

When we were little girls, many of us dreamt of being rescued from our mundane life by Prince Charming, who would whisk us off to a castle to live happily ever after.

While the apostle Peter, in 1 Peter 2:9, doesn't talk about Prince Charming or castles, he does talk about royalty. This is the royalty we inherit as daughters of the King, and he explains how this knowledge should mold, shape, and drive our worth and identity.

Peter tells this to his friends, but we could use the reminder too. Peter was a close friend and follower of Jesus who knew the pain of failure. When things were heating up, and Jesus was arrested, Peter denied even knowing Jesus. Peter could have lived in the failure and shame of the past. He could've allowed names like "failure", "coward", "backstabber", or "weak" to define him and clothe him with shame.

But he didn't... he wrote these words in a letter to some of the early members of the church, encouraging them to live strong amid intense persecution.

To have hope because of Jesus.

To not give in to the labels and names people are trying to put on them.

To not be pressed into someone else's mold.

Here's what he tells them... *"But you are a chosen people, a royal priesthood, a holy nation, God's special possession, that you may declare the praises of him who called you out of darkness into his wonderful light."* 1 Peter 2:9

You are a *chosen people.*

As a child, I remember having to choose teams during PE class. I dreaded standing there awkwardly while the best athletes were chosen first (which, by the way, was never me). Still, to this day, I vividly remember being one of the last picked for a kickball team. Painful.

Don't worry. God hasn't forgotten you or left you out. He has chosen you. In fact, you were His first-round draft pick!

You are a *royal priesthood.*

When my daughters were young, they talked about being Disney princesses who rode beautiful horses and wore fancy gowns. They wore their princess costumes daily anywhere I would let them.

Being "royal", however, isn't something you choose to become; you must be born into a royal family. Those born into royalty receive special privileges, high honor, abundant provision, and lots of protection.

In Christ, you *are* royalty. You are a royal daughter of your heavenly King. You represent the kingdom of the God you serve. This is a great privilege, but it's also a great responsibility with an expectation to represent God's kingdom well.

You are a *holy nation.*

Something holy is pure, unstained, undefiled, and without blemish or defect. In Christ, you aren't "almost holy", or "maybe someday you'll be holy", or "really trying to be holy".

In Christ, you *are* holy.

The cloak of shame, the scars of the past, and the bandages of hurt can be cast aside. The shed blood of Jesus Christ, who died on the cross to take away your sin and shame, empowers and enables you to be presented before God as holy.

You are God's *special possession.*

I can't help but think of all the care and concern I give to protect all the Brenes family's *special possessions*: health insurance, life insurance, car insurance, travel insurance, property insurance, keys, passwords, padlocks, deadbolts, gates, seatbelts, firewalls, fences, security systems…the list goes on and on.

Why? Because these people and items are valuable to me, and I want my special possessions protected.

You, my friend, are God's special possession! You are of immeasurable value to Him. He has engraved your name in the palm of His hand and He even holds all of your tears in a bottle (Isaiah 49:16, Psalm 56:8).

That's how valuable and special you are to God. He takes great care in protecting you, watching over you, and providing for your well-being.

Through Christ, God takes ordinary people and gives them a special status. And with special status comes a special assignment.

What's your *special assignment*? Peter continues to let us know that all God's gracious provision is for a specific reason, *"...that you may declare the praises of him who called you out of darkness into his wonderful light."* (verse 9)

You are a recipient of God's mercy and grace. With all you have received from God—His grace, love, mercy, and goodness—He desires you to live your life declaring the goodness and grace of God to others.

Peter finishes this thought in verse 10, *"Once you were not a people, but now you are the people of God; once you had not received mercy, but now you have received mercy."* 1 Peter 2:10

Once you were not a people...now God considers you, His people. Once you had not received mercy...now because of Jesus, you have received mercy.

Only through Christ is this possible. Only through Christ, can we live differently.

Hold your head high, sister. You are a daughter of the King. You are a recipient of God's mercy and grace.

Take all you have received from God, boldly declare it, and share it with others. Because just as *you* are valuable to God, *all people* are valuable to God.

Wear those fancy hats and gowns with pride.

Day Four – Vessels of Great Worth

I'm going to let you in on a little secret. I'm a pretty good singer. At least, *I* think I am.

The problem is no one agrees with me. I think I sound good… in my head. My family would probably concede that I'm a decent carpool-karaoke singer. I can belt out *Party in the USA* like very few can.

Here's the thing. I'm average in a lot of things. Not great. Just average. And there have been seasons in my life when I wondered how, and even why, God would use me when so many people are better talented, more capable, and smarter.

Perhaps that's how you feel. You look at your life and think, *"I'm not special…just average. How could God use me? Why would God use me?"*

Let me assure you this is God's specialty! He's an expert in using broken, imperfect, average people like you and me to accomplish His greater purpose.

Time after time in the scriptures, we see God choosing, not the most educated, talented, or capable, but broken and hurting people who have really messed up to accomplish His purpose.

In the book of Acts, we're introduced to Saul (later in the New Testament, Saul is referred to by his Greek name, Paul). Saul had made a lot of mistakes. He was an enemy of God's people; he persecuted the early followers of Christ and even traveled from city to city, attempting to destroy the church.

But God had a greater purpose for Saul. He saw beyond what Saul had done and looked toward what He could potentially do through Saul.

In Acts 9:15, God gives this ordinary guy, Ananias, the special responsibility to take the message of Jesus to Saul. A scary job considering Saul's reputation, but God assures Ananias that He was at work, *"But the Lord said, 'Go, for Saul is my chosen instrument to take my message to the Gentiles and to kings, as well as to the people of Israel.'"* Acts 9:15

In this scripture, the original Greek word for *instrument* is *skeuos*, meaning *a vessel*. Vessels are containers; they hold stuff. God is describing Saul as his *chosen vessel*, someone whom He handpicked to carry the message of the Good News of the Gospel.

If you've received Jesus Christ as your Lord and Savior, your body is a container for the Holy Spirit (1 Corinthians 6:19-20).

133

What precious cargo dwells inside of you! Shouldn't your life reflect this incredible worth by how you care for yourself?

God can use any vessel. It doesn't have to be a fancy or fashionable vessel. However, to be most effective in carrying God's precious message, God's vessels need to be clean and emptied of the clutter that can confuse His message.

As women, we can become so busy taking care of everybody else that we neglect to take care of ourselves. How can we realistically expect to reflect God's likeness if our spirits are depleted, and our bodies are run down and worn out?

Perhaps you're wondering, *"Where do I even begin?"*

Take small steps forward. Small, simple steps taken consistently will produce lasting growth and change. Here are two practical places to start.

Stay close to God.

It's difficult to tell others about your relationship with God if you don't have an active, growing relationship with God. It sounds like a no-brainer, yet this is often what we attempt to do.

We read a book, go to church, small group, or Bible study so someone else can tell us about God. But how much time do we spend cultivating our relationship with God? Spending daily time with Him simply because we enjoy His presence?

When you're going through a difficult time, where do you turn? A bag of Oreos? The TV? Social Media? Or to God? I admit that I've been known to say "Yes" to all the above.

Consistent, daily time spent with God through reading your Bible and praying will not only fill you with God's spirit and strengthen you, but it will also produce an eternal change in your life. Your attitudes, thought patterns, and behavior begin to change as you fill yourself with the Word and surrender your heart to Him.

The Creator God wants to spend time with YOU! He sees value in being with YOU!

Take care of your spiritual health by setting aside time *every day* to cultivate your relationship with God. No one else can do that for you. A life lived close to God will reflect God's likeness in love, care, and service to others. People will be drawn to you, not because you're perfect, but because they see something special in how you relate to God and people.

Stay with a healthy diet and exercise.

Ok...before you dismiss this section and skip ahead to the next one, stick with me for a minute. In Romans 12, Paul gives the Roman Christians some instructions for healthy living. Here's what he tells them,

"So here's what I want you to do, God helping you: Take your everyday, ordinary life—your sleeping, eating, going-to-work, and walking-around life—and place it before God as an offering. Embracing what God does for you is the best thing you can do for him. Don't become so well-adjusted to your culture that you fit into it without even thinking. Instead, fix your attention on God. You'll be changed from the inside out. Readily recognize what he wants from you, and quickly respond to it. Unlike the culture

around you, always dragging you down to its level of immaturity, God brings the best out of you, develops well-formed maturity in you." Romans 12:1-2, The Message

God doesn't ban fast food or require us to spend an hour a day at the gym. But the Bible does instruct us to live with the purpose and intention of honoring God with our lives.

Under the Mosaic Law, the Jewish people were required to offer various animal sacrifices to God. In this passage, Paul explains that they are to live differently.

Because of Jesus, we no longer offer animal sacrifices. But God asks us – out of obedience and because of His gracious provision through Jesus – to offer ourselves, our lives set apart for service to Him and other people.

I'm not saying you need to join CrossFit or commit to the Keto diet, but simply pray and ask God what small step He might ask you to take. Because in God's eyes, you're not "just average". You are valuable, and He desires to use your life as His chosen vessel to show other people their value.

You are His chosen vessel, and He desires to work through your lives to accomplish His purpose. Your response should be to live in such a way that you honor God to reflect His high value.

Just as artists sign their paintings to mark their masterpieces, God has marked you. God wants to use your life to display His glory, significance, and presence in the world.

Day Five – God's Answer to a Hurting World

Years ago, when Gregg and I undertook the challenge of restoring two of my grandmother's old, mid-century chairs, we didn't begin the project by slapping a fresh coat of paint on them.

It was a carefully detailed process.

First, we removed all the old fabric, reducing the chairs down to their bare frames. Then, Gregg thoroughly stripped and sanded the chairs down to the bare wood, removing all traces of the previous stain and varnish.

It was a long, meticulous process of eliminating the old before we added the new. But once completed, you could see the beauty of the chairs shine through and appreciate the original design of the furniture.

God's restoration process in our lives isn't surface-level or cosmetic; He works from the inside out. As we allow Him to strip away the old and restore our lives, something beautiful happens – we grow in our capacity to appreciate the beauty God deposited into others.

This ability to impart value to others is truly one of the most precious gifts God has given to us as His children. Our compassion for others should set us apart as followers of Christ.

Unfortunately, this isn't always the case. Because our hearts are selfish and drawn to sin, Christ's followers can sometimes be self-centered, judgmental, and critical. I'm embarrassed to admit that, at times, I've been guilty as well.

Friends, allow me to share a little secret with you – a me-centered life will lead to misery. A full life is experienced when we extend our life to others, not shrink into solitude.

When my eyes focus outward, and my heart opens to be used by God, I'm able to see the world through a completely different lens – one that places a premium on people, seeing them not as an inconvenience or interruption, but with the care and compassion of Jesus.

Jesus modeled this example to us. While He cared for everyone, the Gospel writers consistently draw attention to His care for the oppressed and outcasts in society. Jesus was so different from the other religious leaders of His time. He continually gave value to the "unvalued" of Hebrew people. He was an advocate for the oppressed and underprivileged; He crossed all cultural and class boundaries, comforted all people, and valued everyone.

"When he saw the crowds, he had compassion on them, because they were harassed and helpless, like sheep without a shepherd. ³⁷ Then he said to his disciples, 'The harvest is plentiful but the workers are few. ³⁸ Ask the Lord of the harvest, therefore, to send out workers into his harvest field.'" Matthew 9:36-38

God's answer to the hurting people in the world? YOU!

You are Valuable

When Jesus encountered people, He saw an invitation to make an impact, not an inconvenience to his schedule.

Jesus didn't withdraw from crowds; He drew near to them.

Crowds of people didn't frustrate Jesus; He emanated compassion – a deep sympathy for their brokenness and a compelling desire to alleviate their suffering.

Your life is valuable to God, and you have the presence of the Holy Spirit dwelling inside of you. God has given you an indescribable gift of having the ability to impart value to others.

Growing with compassion, your me-centered day becomes others-oriented, full of potential with hope that God would use you to enfold His hurting children with the love of Jesus.

God says you are of great value to Him. Your response should be to live in such a way that you honor God and reveal to others their high value and worth in God's eyes.

8

You are Secure

Day One – Security Blankets

Things were just better for Brandon when he had his blankie with him. The dark wasn't as scary, boo-boos didn't hurt as much, and staying with a babysitter didn't take as much of an emotional toll on him. When he felt uneasy, it comforted him; when he was scared, it calmed his fears; when he was tired, it gave him peace.

Our son, Brandon, dragged his blanket around like Linus from the *Peanuts* gang. As the years passed, it grew old and tattered, but his love and devotion to his blankie remained strong. That is, until that fateful day when he placed it on the hot stove shortly after I had finished cooking.

Don't be too alarmed – we didn't have to call the Fire Department. There were no *open* flames, just a smoldering, smoky smell wafting in the air. But from then on, Brandon's much-loved white blankie resembled a charred, overcooked marshmallow.

That day, Brandon burned his security blanket. It was an emotional moment for our little guy. He couldn't bear to imagine life without his beloved blankie! But something about the finality of it was liberating for him.

While you're probably not dragging a blanket around with you, do you have some "security blankets" that maybe it's time for you to burn?

Where do you look for your security?

Something secure is firmly fixed and not easily shaken or destroyed. The ability of any structure to stand firm depends on the foundation upon which it is built. If the foundation of a building is flawed, fractured, or too shallow, the building (no matter how beautiful it may appear) won't likely remain standing when a powerful storm hits.

When we lived in Los Angeles, there was always an awareness that an earthquake could strike at any moment. For this reason, tall buildings in Southern California are built upon rolling foundations dug deep into the ground.

I vividly remember being at a women's retreat when a fairly large earthquake struck in the middle of the night. NOT a pleasant way to wake up!

As I prayed and held on for dear life, the hotel in which I was staying felt like a boat rolling over waves on the ocean. Although a frightening experience, the building's solid foundation stood strong through the rolling, jolting, and shaking.

In Luke 6:47-49, Luke gives the example of two homes built on different foundations.

"As for everyone who comes to me and hears my words and puts them into practice, I will show you what they are like. [48] They are like a man building a house, who dug down deep and laid the foundation on rock. When a flood came, the torrent struck that house but could not shake it, because it was well built. [49] But the one who hears my words and does not put them into practice is like a man who built a house on the ground without a foundation. The moment the torrent struck that house, it collapsed and its destruction was complete." Luke 6:47-49

Notice Luke doesn't say *if* a flood comes; he says *when* a flood comes. All of us will experience floods; we all will experience difficult situations that will challenge our faith. All of us will experience seasons where our life is shaken and the foundation upon which we have built our life is revealed. Our ability to weather these impending storms depends on the foundation we have built our life.

One commentary noted that "both houses looked the same from the outside; but they were far different because of their foundation."[1]

God created us to live securely and confidently in Him. He is Truth, and He alone is the Rock upon which we can build secure lives that will remain strong and firmly fixed through rough, uncertain, and stormy times.

Our true security, identity, and sense of worth are found as we grow in our knowledge of God and our confidence that He loves us and is with us during the storm. No matter how messed up or stressed out your life may be, you can be secure and at peace because God loves you, He is with you, and He desires to be glorified through your life.

It all starts with digging deep into God's Word. Getting to know His character gives us confidence and assurance that we can trust Him to carry us through the storms and floods of life.

Things may be falling apart all around you. You may feel as if you're drowning in the rising floodwaters. But your hope, faith, and security can be anchored in the constant, unchanging rock-solid truth that God is good, He is faithful, He loves you, He is for you, and He is with you.

Day Two – The Best Place Ever

Probably the most significant contributor to the insecurity I've experienced in my life is the haunting fear that people won't approve of me or accept me. Time and time again, I've retreated in the face of fear.

Fear of failing...

Fear of being rejected...

Fear of the unknown...

Fear of not being enough, knowing enough, having enough, achieving enough...

Fear. Fear! FEAR!

Fear weighs us down like a sack of bricks, hindering us from stepping out, moving forward, and trusting God.

The enemy will use any opportunity to remind us of where we have failed, where we're insufficient and coming up short.

Every time you're passed up for a promotion, overlooked for a position, fail at a new business venture, receive a poor grade, left out of a get-together, start a new job, receive correction, or don't receive as many "likes" on social media as someone else, you may sense your security shake and fear arise.

Insecurity says you'll never fit in. You'll never be good enough. Nobody loves or appreciates you, so why even try?

On the contrary, God affirms our worth and reminds us that we're valuable and loved.

God doesn't want fear and insecurity to control our lives. He longs for us to walk in the security and confidence He created for us to enjoy. When we are secure in who God has made us to be and content where He has placed us, then we can fulfill what He's created us to do.

Another byproduct – our relationships are so much richer, fuller, and more satisfying because we're not looking to other people or accomplishments to give us what only God can provide.

He created you to be secure, and He created you to be confident, and He desires for you to know you're cared for and precious in His sight.

As Paul explained to the Corinthian church, *"This means that anyone who belongs to Christ has become a new person. The old life is gone; a new life has begun!"* 2 Corinthians 5:17 NLT

This is great news for followers of Christ! When God looks at you, He doesn't see your flaws, weaknesses, and failures; He sees a new person made in the precious likeness of Jesus.

Think about this – if our lives are built on the secure foundation of Jesus and His truth, and God sees us as a new person – pure and righteous, why do we continue to struggle with such deep-rooted insecurity?

I've noticed that when I'm feeling insecure, most of the time it's because my focus has shifted. Instead of focusing on God and His ability to provide and protect me, I'm more concerned about my ability to look good or to control and accomplish things.

146

When things are going well, I can easily say that I'm secure and trust God. But when things in my life are uncertain, relationships are strained, and the future is unknown, the cracks in my life are revealed as I begin grasping for stability wherever I can find it.

Addressing the nation of Israel, Isaiah speaks of the future peace and security they will someday enjoy through the coming Messiah by giving a vibrant illustration of what it looks like to be secure.

"This is what the Lord says: 'I will give Jerusalem a river of peace and prosperity. The wealth of the nations will flow to her. Her children will be nursed at her breasts, carried in her arms, and held on her lap. [13] I will comfort you there in Jerusalem as a mother comforts her child.'" Isaiah 66:12-13 NLT

In this passage, God compares His children to infants being nursed and carried in their mothers' arms. Can you think of anything more secure than a baby resting and being nursed in the arms of its mother?

In their mommy's arms is where they feel loved, provided for, at rest, and secure. It's where they can be comforted from all their fears, feel safe, and be at peace.

Theologian John Calvin wrote concerning this passage in Isaiah, "in order to express more strongly His affection towards us, He compares himself to a mother, whose love exceeds every other by a wide margin. The Lord wishes to be like a mother to us, so that instead of annoyances, reproaches, distresses, and anxieties

147

that we have endured, He may treat us gently and, as it were, fondle us in His bosom."[2]

The best and most secure place ever is found in the arms of God. It's the place where fear dissipates, anxiety is diminished, and insecurity is uprooted.

When you are secure, you can be fruitful and flourish in whatever God is calling you to do. Your confidence is rooted – not in your circumstances, not in who does or doesn't like you – but in God, and you are focused on pursuing Him with undivided, undistracted devotion.

In doing so, others can see the love and faithfulness of God. People can see how God truly created us to live. And others will be drawn and inspired to live this way.

Day Three – I Don't Wanna Make Friends Again

It's funny how certain environments and experiences have a way of revealing the insecurity that's already in our hearts.

I remember being pregnant with our fourth child – due to give birth any day – when we moved to a new city. (Not something I recommend, by the way.) As much as I wanted to be excited about Gregg's new job and the new opportunity, I longed for the familiarity of what we left behind. I missed my house, my friends, and my grocery store.

Would I be able to make new friends with four young kids? Would I be able to find my way to Target without getting lost? Would this place ever feel like home?

Maybe you currently find yourself in a season when things are changing, unfamiliar, and your future is unknown.

You're in between jobs.

You just got married.

Your marriage has ended.

You're moving to a new city.

You just had a baby.

Your kids moved out, and your home is eerily quiet.

You received an unsettling message from your doctor.

Your health is changing.

You're changing.

When things in our life change, it shakes us. Sometimes it shakes us so hard that we don't know where to start to begin moving forward again.

Over the years, I've discovered the secret to moving forward. Ready to hear it?

Take a step.

Then one more step.

And another step.

Moving forward starts by taking small steps, all while anchoring your life deep in God's Word, trusting His strength to sustain you and His wisdom to lead you.

Some experiences we all will face at one time or another possess the ability to shake our security. As we read a couple of days ago, it's not a matter of *"if"* the shaking happens but *"when"*. Anchoring your life in the right thing enables you to weather the storm when it hits.

The writer of Hebrews points us to our anchor for hope. *"We have this hope as an anchor for the soul, firm and secure. It enters the inner sanctuary behind the curtain, [20] where our forerunner, Jesus, has entered on our behalf."* Hebrews 6:19-20

We can have deep confidence in this present life because of the hope of our future eternal life secured for us through the blood of Jesus.

Regardless of the shaking and instability that sometimes surrounds us on earth, our future eternal security is guaranteed. That's where we need to fix our eyes. That's our hope. That's the firm and fixed anchor for our souls.

In these next few days, we'll look at common areas that tend to trip us up, shake our security, and cause us to doubt, become paralyzed, worry, and feel unsure of ourselves. Let's start by considering how transitions and change have a way of unearthing desperate insecurity in us.

Transitions...

Transitions are tough. Having moved a lot (15 times in our married life and many more as a college/young adult). I've experienced firsthand how transitions affect security.

Moving to a new city, attending a new school, starting a new job, and even joyful transitions such as getting married and having a baby force us out of our comfort zone into new and unfamiliar territory.

When our "normal" world is suddenly turned upside down, and we're faced with new people, unfamiliar surroundings, and often-uncomfortable circumstances, our security can be shaken to its core.

There's something safe about things staying the same, isn't there? Change is challenging, but it provides a unique environment for God to work in our life.

When our family was preparing for another cross-country move, I remember hitting an emotional wall one night. Overwhelmed, I remember sobbing and sharing with Gregg, *"I don't want to make friends again!"*

The uncertainty was paralyzing. Yet, this transition – like the ones before and the ones since – forced me to step out of my comfort zone and trust God in a greater way.

God became real to me in ways I hadn't experienced because the places I had normally looked for security had been taken away. It was a difficult season, and it took time to adjust, but I saw God's faithfulness to provide for everything I needed.

Through every transition, whether a major move, a new job opportunity, or the birth of a child, God has been completely faithful to meet every longing and need. He has been a refuge, a source of strength, and a dear friend.

I love how the psalmist describes God's loving care for us through the seasons of uncertainty and change. *"The Lord himself watches over you! The Lord stands beside you as your protective shade. ⁶ The sun will not harm you by day, nor the moon at night. ⁷ The Lord keeps you from all harm and watches over your life. ⁸ The Lord keeps watch over you as you come and go, both now and forever."* Psalm 121:5-8 NLT

The Lord watches over you. He protects you, leads you, and guides you through every transition you may face. You are never alone. He is your strength, security, and source of stability and satisfaction through every transition.

It's in Him we find our true security and worth.

Day Four – Don't Embarrass Me, Mom

Our youngest child is almost finished with high school. (Excuse me while I cry and drown my sorrow in a bag of chocolate chip cookies).

A while back, we attended one of those beginning-of-the-year things at her school. On the way there, Jessica pleaded with Gregg and me not to– under ANY circumstances – ask her friends embarrassing questions. To what could she possibly be referring? We're the cool parents, right?

She persisted and referred to an "awkward conversation" Gregg had with one of her close friends when he asked her about her skincare regimen.

A reasonable question, right?! I mean, she has very nice skin.

Jessie continued by saying she hopes to be friends with some of these people, and she'd prefer if we don't risk it for her by making things more complicated than they have to be. This leads to another experience that can rattle our security...

Relationships...

During much of my youth and young adult life, my security was inordinately anchored in having the right friends and making sure people liked me. I worked hard to impress people, trying to at least appear like I had my life together.

I thought I'd feel secure if I had many friends. But I didn't. I was desperately looking for approval and affirmation. My drive to please everyone was like running on a treadmill. I wore myself out but didn't get anywhere.

I'd worry about conversations and over-analyze interactions because I was afraid they wouldn't want to be my friend if they really knew me. And on the occasion when tension did arise in the friendship, it would crush me, and I'd determine not to be so vulnerable the next time.

I've come a long way, but I'm by no means immune to how friendships can affect my security.

When we make ourselves vulnerable to people, we open our hearts to potentially being hurt. The answer isn't to harden our heart or erect walls to protect ourselves. Instead, we're invited to learn how to trust God and anchor our security in His love and faithfulness.

In the Old Testament, David pours out his heart to God in a desperate season that left him feeling lonely and afraid. People were chasing him. He was living life on the run and hiding in caves for the better part of fifteen years. All because his best friend's dad was jealous of him and wanted him dead!

If anyone had reason to crawl into a cave and disengage from the world, David did. But he didn't. In fact, many of the psalms recorded in the Old Testament were written by David during this desperate and lonely season he endured.

In Psalm 56, we see the anguish in David's soul, but we also see his declaration of trust in God and his unwavering hope that God is with him amid the darkness surrounding him.

"You keep track of all my sorrows. You have collected all my tears in your bottle. You have recorded each one in your book. [9] My enemies will retreat when I call to you for help. This I know: God is on my side! [10] I praise God for what he has promised; yes, I praise the Lord for what he has promised. [11] I trust in God, so why should I be afraid? What can mere mortals do to me?" Psalm 56:8-11 NLT

Our relationship with Christ is the one relationship in which we can anchor our lives. When other relationships leave us battered and bruised, He knows your pain.

When others reject you, Jesus is always there.

When your friends betray you, He is on your side.

When those you love are unfaithful and untrustworthy, He is the One in whom you can trust and place your confidence.

Yet, another thing that can rattle our security…

Who God created me to be…

I've heard that even supermodels have aspects of their appearance they don't like and wish they could change.

Former Victoria's Secret model Cameron Russell describes it this way, *"If you ever are wondering, 'If I have thinner thighs and shinier hair, will I be happier?' you just need to meet a group of models, because they have the thinnest thighs and the shiniest hair and the coolest clothes, and they're the most physically insecure women on the planet."* [3]

While everyone has certain parts of their appearance or personality traits they would change, our security must be anchored deeper than our skin.

God created you with the specific looks and talents you possess for a purpose. You may not care much for your height, eye color, body shape, nose shape, the sound of your voice, or some other physical limitation. But your imperfections don't limit God, nor do they hinder Him from using you.

When anointing the next king of Israel, God reminds the prophet, Samuel, that He has a different grid to determine someone's ability to be used by God.

"But the Lord said to Samuel, 'Do not consider his appearance or his height, for I have rejected him. The Lord does not look at the things people look at. People look at the outward appearance, but the Lord looks at the heart.'" 1 Samuel 16:7

Our weaknesses – physical appearance and limitations – keep us humble and dependent on God while also providing an avenue for God to be glorified through our lives. In our weakness, we begin to experience God's grace and power working through us in a greater way.

If we had it all together, we wouldn't really need God and probably wouldn't seek Him or depend on Him. Our default security would be in ourselves and not in the God who created us for a relationship with Him.

God created you just the way you and you bring Him great pleasure. While the world places a lot of emphasis on our outward appearance, God looks deeper – into the heart.

Your security doesn't come from your relationships or appearance. It's rooted in the unchanging truth that God loves you just the way you are.

Day Five – Times and Seasons

As a single adult, I watched many friends walk down the aisle and looked forward to the day I'd be married. As a newly married woman, I would watch young moms caring for their littles and long to have a baby. Then as a young mom, I envied the wisdom and apparent freedom (they had me fooled) of older moms. Now as an older mom, every so often, I find myself desiring to venture back to those earlier seasons of my life.

Perhaps one week tucked somewhere in my mid-thirties when I was the perfect age, in the perfect season of life, with everything *just perfect*?!

I don't think I'm alone in this. There's something in us that longs for what once was or what we hope will someday be. The problem is that doing so can rob us of the joy and beauty of the present season. Your season of life can shake your security.

Season of life…

Centuries ago, King Solomon wrote about the different seasons of life. Let's reflect on two verses found in Ecclesiastes 3.

"For everything there is a season, a time for every activity under heaven… Yet God has made everything beautiful for its own time." Ecclesiastes 3:1, 11 NLT

There is a time and a season for everything. You can have confidence knowing God will bless and make everything beautiful that is done in His timing and for His purpose.

Discontentment can sneak in and unexpectedly rob us of our security in Christ.

Young moms who feel insignificant because they are not working in the professional world; single women despairing because they are not yet married.

Married women who are discontent because they do not yet have children.

Older women who desire to be and look younger.

Younger women who want to be treated with the respect of older women.

New moms longing for the flexibility of life (and sleep) before children.

The list is endless!

While it's not wrong to desire some of these things, we can't allow them to steal God's significance and importance for us *right now*. If God didn't have a great purpose and treasure for you in your current season of life, He would change it!

He notices *every* detail of your life. Even when you're feeling overwhelmed, tired, spread too thin, unappreciated, or unnoticed, there is a God who sees you and is with you when nobody else is.

Every dish you wash, every sock you fold, every expense report you file, every carpool you drive, and every diaper you change is an opportunity to glorify God – not because the task is noble, but your life, offered in service to God is.

God offers you unique opportunities to glorify Him even in the routine of life because He sees everything you do—even the little, every day, and seemingly mundane things.

God wants you to know that you can trust Him. The season of life you are currently in is rich with purpose, significance, and potential. Don't spend so much time complaining about your current season that you miss experiencing the treasures God has for you right now.

Potential failure can also affect our security…

Failure…

We naturally derive a lot of our worth and security from our accomplishments and are often unaware we're doing so until we fail or something goes awry. While it's not enjoyable to experience failure, it's part of life. It's also a great opportunity to learn something valuable if we're willing to yield to God and His work in our life.

We can learn and grow from our failures, or they can be places where we become stuck. Although God loves us, He doesn't guarantee that we'll win every game, ace every test, or receive every job for which we apply.

We will fail. We will make mistakes.

Failure shouldn't hinder us from trying great things and shouldn't paralyze us from attempting new things. Those who are secure in Christ can admit when they have messed up and made mistakes. They're quick to say sorry and refrain from making excuses and blaming others. They evaluate, adjust, and move forward.

The apostle Paul was a man who knew hardship and failure. But he also knew there was a greater lesson to be learned within the difficulty. In his letter to the Corinthian church, he shares with them the troubles he was facing.

"We do not want you to be uninformed, brothers and sisters, about the troubles we experienced in the province of Asia. We were under great pressure, far beyond our ability to endure, so that we despaired of life itself. [9] Indeed, we felt we had received the sentence of death. But this happened that we might not rely on ourselves but on God, who raises the dead. [10] He has delivered us from such a deadly peril, and he will deliver us again. On him we have set our hope that he will continue to deliver us..."
2 Corinthians 1:8-10

When things are going well, our natural tendency is to drift. If everything is always *up and to the right*, why would we trust God? We could do it on our own.

Hardships, pain, and failure – while never pleasant – build our faith and teach us to rely on God.

Set your hope on God and Him alone. He is the One who orders our steps, grants us success, and makes us secure. He promises to be with us every step of the way.

Day Six – What's Next?

Ok, consider this a bonus devotional this week because this last one is a biggie. Not knowing what the future holds can be unsettling. If you're a planner like me, it can be downright terrifying. Are you ready to see how the unknown can shake our security?

The unknown...

Things that have kept me up at night – paying for college, saving for retirement, financial issues, health issues, kid issues, relational issues, and moving our family...just to name a few.

When we sold our house in Nashville, we had no definitive plans regarding our next step. We sensed it was time for something new but didn't know what *"new"* would look like or *where* it would take us.

Being the type of person who likes to have everything planned out and figured out, this was difficult and uncomfortable.

I continually asked Gregg, *"What's our plan?" "Where are we going to go?"* and *"How much longer do you think we will be here?"* I am positively sure that I drove him nuts with all my questions.

It was so frustrating for me not to know, not to be in control, not to have a plan, not to have my life neatly mapped out!

Sadly, these unknown seasons reveal a fragile place in my heart. When I'm in control, it's easy to say I trust God, but when I'm facing things I can't control, how settled is my heart?

Through experiences like these, God is teaching me I can trust Him. I'm learning true security comes from surrendering our unknowns and future to God, not by controlling our circumstances and having every detail neatly organized and figured out.

The apostle Paul modeled this beautifully for us. In Acts, with his life in danger, he vulnerably shares about his journey into his unknown future.

"And now, compelled by the Spirit, I am going to Jerusalem, not knowing what will happen to me there. ²³ I only know that in every city the Holy Spirit warns me that prison and hardships are facing me. ²⁴ However, I consider my life worth nothing to me; my only aim is to finish the race and complete the task the Lord Jesus has given me—the task of testifying to the good news of God's grace." Acts 20:22-24

If the Holy Spirit warned me that prison and hardships were in my near future, you'd probably find me locking my doors and windows and hiding under my covers. I'd love to say confidently that I'd move forward with determined faith in God. But honestly, I'm pretty sure I'd be scared.

Paul is a great example for us. He determined not to waste his time worrying about what may or may not happen to him.

He lived his life with a greater purpose and focus – to know God and share His love with others. His foundation was so rock solid that he remained unshaken - even though jail, suffering, and eventual death were in his inevitable future.

Paul's security came from a life that was surrendered to God in a loving relationship, and he trusted the Lord to take care of him and help him navigate the unknown elements of his life.

Because Paul was secure in Christ, God was able to use him to reach and influence many people. He wasn't preoccupied with what people thought of him. He didn't fear failure or the uncertainty of the future. People were drawn to him and desired to know the God that had radically transformed his life.

Our security is built upon the foundation of Jesus – knowing Him, knowing He loves us, and knowing who He has created us to be. As you allow the Word of God to define you and transform you, He will cause you to stand firm and secure in who He created you to be, through relationships, different seasons of life, transitions, failures, and the unknown parts of your life.

Surrender all your cares to God. You can trust Him and rest secure in His presence. As the psalmist declared, *"Your favor, O Lord, made me as secure as a mountain."* Psalm 30:7 NLT

9

You are Accepted

Day One – It Stings

During a recent parent-teacher open house at my kids' high school, I visited with Justin's Japanese teacher. After a few minutes of exchanging pleasantries, we discussed my child's progress when the unthinkable occurred.

Out of nowhere, a gigantic bee made a beeline (yes, pun *very* intended) straight for my head! My attempts to shoo it away and dodge its path failed and the bee landed on my neck, giving me a potent sting.

Our composed parent-teacher discussion quickly shifted to shrieks and shrills as my husband and this wonderful teacher attempted to remove the large stinger protruding from my neck. The growing line of parents waiting to have their moment with the teacher stood and stared while the teacher rushed to apply an ice pack and Band-Aid to a grateful but embarrassed patient.

Hopefully, you haven't been stung by a bee at a parent/teacher open house, but I'm pretty sure you know what it's like to experience the sting of something even more painful – the sting of rejection. It's impossible to journey through life without experiencing the isolating feeling of being rejected, betrayed, and left out.

All of us have felt the pain of being unaccepted, unworthy, or rejected. Go ahead…fill in the blanks.

It's the disappointment of…

It's being excluded from…

It's not being invited to…

It's being overlooked for…

It's not being appreciated by…

Our desire to be loved and accepted is a real need in our lives. It can wound us deeply when it doesn't come from the people and places we expect.

Years ago, Gregg and I were invited to a party. We were so excited to attend. Many of our friends were planning to go, and it was looking to be such a fun evening.

Until we received a call.

Apparently, they had "over-invited". They graciously explained their awkward dilemma – they didn't have enough room in their current venue and needed to "cut back" their guest list.

Guess who didn't make the cut? Yup, that would be us.

It's painful enough when you're not included, but then to be included only to be later excluded – that's painful *and* embarrassing. I was so hurt. Everything in me wanted to be angry, hold a grudge, and fantasize about someday being invited to an even better party with lots of famous people that these people weren't invited to attend.

My wise husband encouraged me to look beyond the present anger and pain to the greater work of healing and humility God desired to shape inside me through the experience.

When we're hurting, the temptation is to nurse the wound, to give it lots of attention. I believe God desires for us to invite Him into our place of pain so He can bring healing. God longs to heal the hurts rejection has inflicted in your heart.

The natural tendency is to protect our hearts, defend our hearts and erect walls around our hearts. But real growth and healing require us to open our fragile, tender hearts to the only One who can truly heal us.

In Psalm 34:18, David recalls God's faithful, tangible presence he experienced while others betrayed and rejected him. David knew what it was like to be rejected. When he wrote this psalm, he was running for his life. King Saul was out to kill him.

David was hiding in caves and living in exile in foreign countries, trying to stay alive. He knew the loneliness of betrayal; he understood the sting of rejection. He wrote, *"The Lord is close to the brokenhearted and saves those who are crushed in spirit."* Psalm 34:18

In the heartbreak, in the hurt, God is near. He draws close to you in those painful, lonely moments and begins to heal you. And in the healing, a new strength emerges, a deeper understanding of God's love and grace, and an intimacy with Him you wouldn't have experienced otherwise.

But how do we begin to move forward and allow our hearts to trust again when the sting of rejection and betrayal is still a fresh, open wound?

I believe it begins by focusing on what David did and where Paul encouraged the Ephesian church to place their focus. Paul wrote, *"Even before he made the world, God loved us and chose us in Christ to be holy and without fault in his eyes. ⁵ God decided in advance to adopt us into his own family by bringing us to himself through Jesus Christ. This is what he wanted to do, and it gave him great pleasure."* Ephesians 1:4-5 NLT

While others may reject you, God accepts you.

That's where our focus should lie. You aren't an afterthought of God. You're not second class or an accident. You're not left out or on the outside looking in.

God loves you. God chose you. God decided to adopt you into His very own family!

You!

Not because He had to, felt sorry for you, or was obligated to you, but because He wanted to. And get this…it gave Him great pleasure.

Verse 13 continues to say, *…And when you believed in Christ, he identified you as his own by giving you the Holy Spirit, whom he promised long ago.*

He identified you as His own. Take a moment to pause and consider what this means to you and how living this truth could shape your life.

I once read that an average of 2% of the population won't like you, and there's absolutely nothing that you can do about it.[1]

No matter how hard you try, you will not be accepted by everyone. And not everybody's going to like you either. But God has not overlooked you. He has not excluded you or edged you out of his club.

In fact, He *identifies you as His own* and longs to give you His very best.

So instead of spending large amounts of energy and time mourning the fact that we won't be liked by everyone, included in everything, hired for every job, be accepted into every school…why don't we decide to place our focus on the lavish love and approval of our heavenly Father?

Doesn't that sound incredibly more life-giving?

The foundation of your worth is not based on who does or doesn't like you or who approves and affirms you.

It is based on the truth that God has made you acceptable, included you in His family, identified you as His own, and provided a way for you to have a relationship with Him through the blood of Jesus.

When you focus on God's acceptance of you, He removes the sting of rejection and replaces it with the sweetness of His Spirit, which is like honey to your soul.

Day Two – Groupies

Years ago, while picking up my children from school, one of my kids got into the car and promptly announced, "Apparently, I'm in the nerd group!"

I was surprised to discover that at the age of nine, there were already "groups" at elementary school, and kids were assigning each other to them!

As we discussed this phenomenon as a family, my kids began educating me on the social structure of elementary, middle, and high school.

According to my kids, once you're assigned to a "group", that designation stays with you through high school. Very rarely can you move to another group. My kids could recall only a few people who had been able to pull it off.

Over the years, we've watched all our children adjust and find their place in new schools, cities, cultures, and environments. They've been bullied on more than one occasion and have, at times, struggled to fit in and find their place. As a parent, you feel so helpless! Everything in me wanted to arrange playdates for them like I did when they were three years old.

At one time or another, we've all been there. God created us with a desire for significance and a need to belong. He created us to live in community – community with Him and community with others. So when we find ourselves on the outside looking in, it can be a lonely and isolating experience.

Maybe that's why I love this story in Luke so much. Let's read it together,

"While Jesus was in one of the towns, a man came along who was covered with leprosy. When he saw Jesus, he fell with his face to the ground and begged him, "Lord, if you are willing, you can make me clean." [13] Jesus reached out his hand and touched the man. "I am willing," he said. "Be clean!" And immediately the leprosy left him. [14] Then Jesus ordered him, "Don't tell anyone, but go, show yourself to the priest and offer the sacrifices that Moses commanded for your cleansing, as a testimony to them." [15] Yet the news about him spread all the more, so that crowds of people came to hear him and to be healed of their sicknesses." Luke 5:12-15

Luke tells us the man was *covered* in leprosy. Think about this man's condition and how it may have affected his sense of worth and feeling of acceptance.

Leprosy is a disease affecting the skin and nerves. The disease destroys the nerve endings and makes its victim unable to sense or feel anything. Sores break out on the skin, and the smell is horrible when they begin to ulcerate. Those diagnosed with leprosy were declared "unclean" in the Jewish culture and they were forbidden to live in the community. They were outcasts and even those who touched them would be considered unclean as well.[2]

This man approaches Jesus and makes a statement, *"If you are willing, you can make me clean..."*

Notice that he didn't say, *"If you are able..."* This man had lived as an outcast — unloved, unwanted, unaccepted, and avoided by people. He wasn't questioning Jesus's ability. He was concerned about Jesus' willingness to help him.

Perhaps his internal dialogue went something like this,

"Who would care about me? Who would want to help someone like me? Why would Jesus be good to me?"

Then a little courage emerges, *"I have nothing to lose, so I'll at least ask."*

I love the fact that Jesus touched this man *before* he cleansed him. He wasn't afraid of the mess; He didn't avoid this man's mess. Instead, Jesus drew near and accepted him just as He was.

While he was still unclean, still an outcast, still unacceptable, Jesus received him, accepted him, and joined him by becoming unclean Himself *before* He healed him. Amazing!

Sometimes I think it's easier to believe in God's goodness for others than to believe it for myself. I know God loves, provides and cares for others, but would He really do that for me?

For us to truly shift from living for the acceptance of others to this secure place of God's acceptance of us, we must grow in believing God's goodness doesn't just extend to everyone else.

Understanding and embracing God's acceptance is coming to a place where I believe God is caring and good *to me* too.[3]

While we may not have leprosy, our story isn't much different from the leper. Romans 5:6-8 says, *"while we were still sinners, Christ died for us"*. In our uncleanliness, pain, and ugliness, Jesus extends His love to touch and heal our lives.

This is significant. We don't have to clean up, fix ourselves, prove our worth, or earn a place with God. He accepts us just as we are...mess and all.

Paul explains to the Ephesian believers how they were once excluded, on the outside and far away from God. The invitation is to come as we are – junk and all – to be a new people, united together with Him through the blood of Jesus (Ephesians 2:12-13).

Chosen and accepted by God. Invited to become *His people*...that's the best "group" we could ever be invited to be associated with.

Day Three – Who are You Afraid of?

It was our oldest daughter's first day at her new middle school. We had moved from Tennessee to Hawaii just two weeks before. She knew no one. No friends. Far away from everything that had been familiar and friendly to her.

And did I mention she was starting *middle school*?

I can't begin to tell you how painful it was for me to see her get out of the car that first day. The dread on her face and the drag in her step was difficult to watch. I knew if she could make just *one* friend, her perspective would begin to change, and this unfamiliar place would begin to feel like home.

Our desire for relationships is an inborn longing God created us to have. It's completely normal for us to seek life-giving friendships. They're essential for our spiritual growth. However, when we look to our relationships to fulfill needs in our life that only God can truly fulfill, problems will arise.

In John 12:42-43, we're told that while many people believed in Jesus, they were afraid to publicly admit it because of what following Jesus would cost them. John writes, *"...they would not openly acknowledge their faith for fear they would be put out of the synagogue; 43 for they loved human praise more than praise from God."* John 12:42-43

174

How sobering to think they compromised their relationship with Jesus because of their desire to receive praise from others!

Yet, how easy is it for me to do the same thing?

"If I share my faith with them, what will they think of me?"

"I want to be invited to their parties, so maybe I should compromise my values just this one time?"

"Everyone at my workplace is doing it. I need to fit in or they may not consider me for the promotion."

"If I say, "no" they won't like me".

While we're called to love people, we shouldn't depend on their praise and acceptance to fill a need in our hearts. Our desire should be to wholeheartedly pursue God and His purpose for our lives, undistracted and unhindered by the reactions of others around us.

Oh, but it can be so hard, especially when we're feeling left out, overlooked, and unappreciated, right?

We have a choice – and it's a choice we won't just make once, but one we must make daily. We can choose to seek God's approval or the approval of others. We can choose to live for the praise of God or for the praise of people. And we can choose to run after God's love for us or run after the love of others.

Before we continue, take an honest look at your heart and ask yourself, *"Whose praise do I seek? Whose acceptance do I crave? Who are the people whom I am currently working to make happy?"*

Go ahead and jot down their names in the margin. I'll wait.

A woman who is secure in God's acceptance will have the courage to choose pleasing God over pleasing people.

Trust me. As a recovering people-pleaser, you will be immensely more effective in fulfilling your purpose when you're confident in God's love and acceptance of you. Running around trying to please everyone and make them happy is exhausting and an impossible task.

Let's get a glimpse of what this looks like in scripture. In the Old Testament, we read about Israel's first king, a man named Saul. God must have seen something special in Saul to choose him for this monumental role in Israel's history. Yet, at some point during his kingship, Saul's ego and desire to be loved and accepted by people interfered with his ability to lead a nation.

In 1 Samuel 15, the prophet Samuel instructs Saul to fight and destroy Israel's enemy, the Amalekites. As Saul leads the Israelites into battle, God gives them a big victory. But instead of destroying everything, Saul decides to keep some of the best stuff for himself and his men. And if this wasn't enough, caught up in the celebration, Saul decides to build a giant monument to honor himself and show everyone how awesome he is.

Samuel is furious, and God regrets making Saul king.

The next day when Samuel visits, Saul proudly assures him that he carried out all the Lord's instructions. Samuel points out that if Saul had truly destroyed *everything*, there wouldn't be all these cattle and sheep around.

Saul defends his actions and makes excuses for his disobedience, blaming his soldiers, claiming the *soldiers* spared the best, and the *soldiers* took the plunder (verse 21).

Finally, after debating with Samuel, Saul admits he was wrong, and we're given a glimpse of the motivation behind his actions.

"Then Saul said to Samuel, 'I have sinned. I violated the LORD's command and your instructions. I was **afraid of the men** *and so I gave in to them.'"* 1 Samuel 15:24 (emphasis mine)

Deep in Saul's heart, he craved the honor of the soldiers more fiercely than the honor that came from God. In his desperate pursuit to gain the support and acceptance of the people, he forfeited his role of leading, loving, and serving them.

If the approval of other people is the primary longing in your heart, it will affect your choices and behavior and hinder God being able to use you to your fullest capacity. You cannot fully, genuinely, and truly love people as God has called you to do if you depend on them to fill an aching need for acceptance in your heart.

This tragic chapter ends with Samuel telling Saul that God is going to take the kingdom of Israel away from him and give it to someone better than him (verse 28).

In contrast, let's jump ahead to 1 Samuel 30 and briefly look at this man, King David, to whom Samuel referred.

"...David and his men arrived home at their town of Ziklag, they found that the Amalekites had made a raid into the Negev and

Ziklag; they had crushed Ziklag and burned it to the ground. ² They had carried off the women and children and everyone else but without killing anyone..." 1 Samuel 30:1-2

How devastating! Everything they had was stolen from them – even their wives and children! Amid his fear, grief, and anger, David had additional problems.

"David was now in great danger because all his men were very bitter about losing their sons and daughters, and they began to talk of stoning him. But David found strength in the LORD his God." 1 Samuel 30:6

One of the things that I love most about David is how he responded in the face of intense betrayal, rejection, and opposition. Saul was a self-seeking, self-serving man who spent much of his kingship not leading a nation and serving the people but chasing after the acceptance of the people.

David responded differently.

Even when his own men—his closest friends—turned against him, David found strength in God. David's heart desired to please and honor the God whom he served. And because of this, his life and leadership looked dramatically different from Saul's.

Oh, if that would be said of us! To be so secure in God's acceptance of us that our eyes are fixed on pleasing him above everything else.

Day Four – Confession Time

I have a confession to make. And honestly, it's something I'm kind of embarrassed to admit. It's easier for me to confess my impatience or a bad attitude, but this one's harder for me to own. (Probably because I feel I should've grown out of it by now.)

It seems just so...*juvenile.*

Okay, I'm just gonna blurt it out...

I find myself – still, at the ripe old age of *(sound of muffled, incoherent large numbers)* – comparing myself with others. And with the ubiquitous presence of social media, there are more ways to do this than ever.

We compare our kids. Jobs. Looks. Health. Bank accounts. Homes. Cars. Social circles. Vacations.

The list could go on forever!

It's been said that comparison is the internal measuring tape we carry around in our back pocket.[4] So true! And if you're as math impaired as I am, you're always coming up short.

Not only is living this way exhausting, but it also takes our focus off our unique gifts and what God has called us to do. God didn't create you to be like your co-worker or your neighbor. He designed you to be the best, most Christ-like version of yourself!

The apostle Paul explains it this way to the Christians in Galatia, *"Pay careful attention to your own work, for then you will get the satisfaction of a job well done, and you won't need to compare yourself to anyone else. ⁵ For we are each responsible for our own conduct."* Galatians 6:4-5 NLT

What a freeing way to live! When we're confident in God's acceptance of us, we'll be focused on what God has called us to do. We're able to take a deep breath and just be ourselves.

God created you unique and different from anyone else. He gave you special gifts, talents, and abilities. He knows you intimately and loves you deeply – just the way you are.

God has chosen you to have a special part in what He is doing in the world. He sees your uniqueness and value and knows you have something special to contribute. You're not an outcast; you're not alone. You belong, and you matter to God.

Don't waste your time and energy trying to be what everyone wants you to be or attempting to be what you think everyone wants you to be. Be the woman God created you to be!

King David seemed comfortable being himself. His passion for God far exceeded his desire to be approved and appreciated by others.

In 2 Samuel 6, David led the procession with dancing and celebration when the Ark of God was being returned to Jerusalem. There was laughing, singing, music swinging, dancing in the street (yes, I just referred to an 80's pop song).[5]

In comparison to his devotion to God, people's opinions of him didn't matter. He had no airs or pretensions, no hidden agendas, or secret motives. David unabashedly worshiped and danced before the Lord, even after being publicly corrected by God in front of the entire nation for improperly transporting the ark.

His wife, however, didn't see things the same way. She couldn't believe her husband, the King of Israel, would act this way (cue: teenage eye-roll) and was embarrassed by his undignified behavior.

I identify with David because I've occasionally been known to get a little *over-excited*. The Italian side of me can be loud, expressive, and passionate, with lots of hand waving and arm movement, while the Japanese side of my husband stares at me as if I've gone a little overboard. My children have been embarrassed by their "over-expressive mother", and I've been told by them on several occasions to *"take it down a notch"*.

Yet our worship of God is the one area where we should feel free to wholeheartedly express our love for Him—unhindered and unrestrained.

Sometimes our concern with what others will think and how people will see us influences our ability to live free in Christ. As a young Christian, I struggled with this. Because I craved approval, I was unable to truly be myself. I often tried to cover up "Kris" and all my flaws, fears, and insecurities. It wasn't authentic or real, and it didn't provide for healthy relationships.

I thought that if people knew me, they might not accept me, and the thought of that scared me. As I've grown in my confidence in God's acceptance of me, I've grown in my ability to be free to be myself.

But it's a process. When you begin living from the place of God's love, you won't depend on it from others.[6]

And when you're not comparing and competing with others, you'll find your heart is at peace and, as Paul instructs... *you will get the satisfaction of a job well done...*

Day Five – Choose Celebrating Over Criticizing

When we left King Saul and Samuel in 1 Samuel 15 (day three), we read that God was grieved that He had made Saul king over Israel. In the next chapter, the prophet Samuel finds a young shepherd named David and anoints him as God's chosen man to replace Saul.

If I were David and I had just been anointed king, I would expect the inauguration to take place soon. God's not happy with the king, another king had been selected, why wait? Come on. Let's get going with it.

Believe it or not, it was over *fifteen years later* when David took the throne as King of Israel. David spent much of those fifteen years hiding in caves and running for his life due to Saul's erratic behavior and jealousy of David.

While waiting that long to see a promise fulfilled would cause many to doubt God, take matters into their own hands or just give up, David used the waiting period as an opportunity to grow stronger in his relationship with God. In fact, he was given two opportunities to end the chaos and kill Saul.

But he didn't. David chose to trust God and His timing instead. He explains in 1 Samuel 26:10-11, *"As surely as the LORD lives," he said, "the LORD himself will strike him, or his time will come and he will die, or he will go into battle and perish.*[11] *But the LORD forbid that I should lay a hand on the LORD's anointed."* 1 Samuel 26:10-11a

Sometimes, our insecurity and need for acceptance can drive us to control our circumstances and become critical of others. Samuel had anointed David king, yet David didn't flaunt about or force his way. He didn't compromise his convictions to make it happen. He didn't criticize Samuel or Saul.

He waited patiently, being confident God would fulfill His plan in His timing.

And because David was secure in God's plan, while he waited, he was able to support Saul's leadership and even celebrate the military success of Israel under Saul's leadership.

Think about this. Saul, the very man who made David's life a miserable mess for over fifteen years…the man who hunted him and forced him to live on the run…the man who stole fifteen years of his time away from his family and friends…the man who deceived him, manipulated him, and attempted to kill him?

David honored and celebrated *him?!*

Yup. David supported Saul's leadership, respected his role, and even celebrated his position as king. David didn't demand fair treatment or seek revenge. He didn't compare or complain. He didn't criticize by telling people how his leadership would be so much better.

He celebrated and served the king whom God had placed in that position for that season. David was so confident in God's plan for his life that he didn't feel threatened by the successes of others.

Oh, that we would be women confident in God's acceptance and lead the way in celebrating the success of others. Unfortunately, in our need to be accepted, our focus can easily shift from being *others-centered* to being *self-centered*. Instead of building bridges to draw others closer, we erect walls to keep others out. We gossip, compete, compare, judge, and criticize – all to make ourselves feel better.

Remember how Jesus responded to the leper in Luke 5? During Jesus' earthly ministry, he served, celebrated, and loved people. His concern wasn't towards *wealthy* people, *pretty* people, *successful* people, or *likable* people; it was for *all* people.

When Jesus saw people, He saw their needs. He felt their hurts and extended to them the love and acceptance of a merciful God. He wasn't jockeying for prominence or high position; He wasn't doing His ministry to be the popular guy. He sought to serve others and let them know they were loved and had value.

I believe it was for one purpose. Paul explains it this way in Romans 15:7, *"Therefore, accept each other just as Christ has accepted you so that God will be given glory."* Romans 15:7 NLT

Did you catch that? Our primary goal in the way we treat people should be to shine a big spotlight on God so He will be glorified. It's not about us.

What a freeing way to live! Instead of allowing your insecurity to hound you with thoughts of not having enough or being enough, celebrate others.

The co-worker who received the promotion you felt you earned? Congratulate them.

The neighbor who took a vacation to a destination you can only dream about going to? Celebrate them.

The friend whose kids are academically and athletically off the chart while your child is in tears doing homework every night? Cheer them on.

The countless friends that are getting married and having babies, and you wonder if it will ever be your turn? Support them.

My friend, accept others, embrace others, celebrate others. Be an encourager! What a simple way for us every day to bring glory to God.

It's so simple, yet…just…so…hard…to…do sometimes!

Let's determine to stop comparing, competing, or contending for something we feel we deserve. And instead, focus outward to others and upward toward Christ.

When we choose to be an extension of God's love by encouraging others, what they think about us shouldn't matter. Our acceptance and worth are found in Christ, not as we bend and conform to what everyone around us wants us to be.

Jesus is for you. He is on your side and wants to use you to impart worth and value to the lives of others. Jesus has accepted you. He has included you as a special, essential part of His family, and He died to set you free.

Free from the opinions of others, free from the approval of others, free from the control of others, and free to be the woman He created you to be.

When we live this way, we shine a big spotlight – not on our awesomeness – but on the amazing God we serve.

10

You are Safe

Day One – Living Free from Fear

Our family enjoys adventure – the thrill, the rush, and the excitement of a challenge just a little beyond us.

While I like the *idea* of adventure, when it comes to extreme danger and high-risk situations, controlled, calculated, and comfortable is more my speed – especially when my kids are involved. When they were little, I would have been perfectly happy if they always had worn bike helmets and swim floaties…just in case.

If you're like me, you understand why my response to my kids' suggestion we go on a family hike was, *"Is it safe?"*

Their exasperated teenage response followed, *"Mooom, it's a short walk along an ocean trail!"*

Just to be sure, I checked the online reviews.

"A nice, easy walk along a coastal path."

It sounded like the perfect hike! Well...you can't believe *everything* on the Internet.

While this *technically* was a coastal path, everyone failed to mention how NARROW this coastal path was as it hugged the ocean shoreline! They also forgot to describe the sheer DROP OFF into the OCEAN upon deviating from this path.

My kids climbed on rocks and leaped along the trail like gazelles prancing through a meadow while I crept along at a turtle's pace, holding a death grip on every rock.

However, even fear couldn't restrain me from shouting my mama warnings,

"Slow down!"

"Watch out!"

"Be careful!"

I'm positive my family enjoyed my delightful company.

As we neared our destination, the only thing standing between us and the beautiful overlook was a seven-foot rock face.

I slumped down on a rock, *"No way! I can't scale that! I'll wait for you here."*

You are Safe

Unable to see beyond the huge obstacle, I shrunk back, deeming the feat impossible.

My kids scampered up undeterred and began shouting,

"Mom, you gotta see this view! It's amazing!"

But *how?* The rock I faced was formidable, and fear's grip fought fiercely to keep my feet firmly on the ground.

"No thanks. I'll. Just. Stay. Put."

Then I thought…

How often do I surrender my desires to fear?

How often do I allow fear to erect an enormous rock between my dreams and me, robbing me of experiencing the joy God created me to live with?

How often do I allow fear to paralyze me and cause me to shrink back and settle for less than I hunger and hope for?

Excuses are my friend when the face of fear balks at me.

In a burst of unexpected faith, I cried, *"Here I come!"*

With a new determination, one step at a time (and with a little help from my husband pushing from behind and my kids pulling me up), I made it to the top…and the view was breathtaking.

Had I stayed on the other side, I would've missed it. And it would've been one more moment when I allowed fear to steal a little piece of joy and freedom from my life.

In Matthew 14:28-29, we see the disciples trembling with fear when they find themselves caught in an unexpected storm. Suddenly Jesus appears, walking on water toward them.

"'Lord, if it's you,' Peter replied, 'tell me to come to you on the water.' ²⁹ 'Come,' he said. Then Peter got down out of the boat, walked on the water and came toward Jesus." Matthew 14:28-29

Jesus didn't calm the storm before He told Peter to step out of the boat. He invited Peter to take a step while the storm was raging.

Jesus must've seen something in Peter that Peter had yet to see in himself. And yes, Peter began to sink, but he took steps anyway. Oftentime, we scorn Peter because he sank. We fail to remember he was the only one brave enough to get out of the boat!

Peter knew to stay in the boat – while more comfortable – wasn't the way he wanted to live. Perhaps he knew the starting place to live free from fear was to take a step toward Jesus.

And by taking a step, Peter got to experience something that just moments earlier he would have probably considered impossible.

Sure, it's scary at first, but with every step we take, we experience a greater freedom and confidence. We also gain a fuller perspective of who God is.

My friend, God placed courage inside of you. Stop allowing fear to guide your steps and chart your course.

Get out of the boat.

Take a step.

Apply for the job.

Sign up for the class.

Make the phone call.

Say "Yes" to the opportunity.

You'll be glad you did.

Freedom is waiting for you on the other side. And by the way, the view is spectacular.

Day Two – We're Gonna Die!

When our family made the massive cross-country, trans-Pacific move from Tennessee to Hawaii many years ago, Gregg and I thought it would be an exciting family adventure to drive our minivan once again across the country…with all our kids…and all our stuff.

It sounded like a good idea *at the time*. How quickly we forgot our travel adventures just two years earlier.

We loaded up our five children and packed our things strategically around them. As the kids contended for their tiny sliver of space, there was barely room to breathe once we shoved the last few stuffed animals and pillows into the car.

While pulling onto I-65 out of Nashville, a friend who witnessed this incredible sight sent us a text saying we looked like the *Beverly Hillbillies*. (Those of you from a younger generation who don't know about the awesomeness of the *Beverly Hillbillies*, you can google them now).

About halfway into our drive, as we were leaving Kansas and approaching the Colorado border, the beautiful weather we were enjoying suddenly changed dramatically. While it was only four in the afternoon, the sky grew eerily dark, and the winds kicked up, becoming so strong you could see several funnel clouds forming in the distance. Although we had only lived in Tennessee for two years, we had quickly learned what tornado weather looked like. This was not a good situation.

To make matters worse, we heard a loud thumping noise on the top of our car. Upon pulling over to investigate, we discovered the noise was coming from the cargo box on top of our car, filled with more of our stuff.

The strong winds had damaged the box, breaking the lock, and was now threatening to fling open and send our stuff flying down the interstate. So here we were, heading into tornado weather with car trouble and no nearby town or exit in sight.

Then, suddenly, very quietly at first, one of our children began to chant softly, *"We're gonna die! We're gonna die! We're gonna die!"* Slowly, each of our kids chimed in, the volume mounted and within minutes, our children were screaming in unison, *"We're gonna die!"*

I looked at Gregg and had one thought, *"We're going to die!"*

Fear can be very contagious.

Thankfully, we didn't die. We made it to the next town, found a friendly neighborhood hardware store, repaired our cargo box, the weather cleared, and we made it safely to Denver for the night.

The experience reminds me of one of my favorite scriptures, *"When I am afraid, I put my trust in you."* Psalm 56:3

Perhaps I love this scripture so much because I need it so often. Notice the scripture doesn't say *"if"* you are afraid, but *"when"* you are afraid. Fear is a very real emotion all of us face. Some fear is good and meant to warn us; some fear isn't good. Either way, fear can remind us to reorient our lives and place our trust in God.

When our life becomes unstable and fear begins to grip us, we're faced with the sudden, uncomfortable realization that our source of safety has been grounded in the wrong place. Instead of trusting that God is with us and will take care of us, fear has a way of overtaking our life and robbing us of the peace God has for us.

Learning to overcome fear has been a major obstacle in my life. As a child, I remember dreading fire prevention week at school. For some reason, all the discussion about fire safety convinced me that my home would burn down that week. I spent the evenings in a sleeping bag on my parent's bedroom floor.

As I outgrew that fear, new ones emerged. I'm not a big fan of uncertainty and I like to feel like I have my life, family, and future under control. I'm learning to trust God in a greater way, but the learning curve is a steep one.

God deeply desires for His children to dwell in the assurance and safety of His care and protection. Despair, disaster, darkness, and danger may, at times, seem to envelop us like a thick blanket. And although we don't always understand what is happening, you can be certain that God is there with you, and He has not abandoned you in your darkest hour.

You are not alone. God promises to protect you and keep you safe. Not only does He watch over you and protect you during your time here on earth, but He also has an eternal place where fear will be gone forever, and you will live safely with Him.

Hopefully, you won't find yourself with car problems in the middle of nowhere in the face of impending tornadoes. Still, you can shift your focus from the darkness and danger surrounding you to the One who has ultimate control over it all.

Day Three – Hey Bear!

As I write this, our family is spending the week in Lake Tahoe, where my in-laws live. This beautiful place has been our home away from home for over twenty-five years and is filled with family memories and experiences.

Today was no exception.

I was out for my morning run when a biker waved me down, urging me to stop. Thankfully, I listened because, within seconds, a big brown bear scampered across the road about 20 yards from me! Startled and stunned, I did what any reasonable person would do. I pulled out my phone to take some photos. I had to have evidence to back up my story to my family!

(During last year's trip, we saw a bear while driving. Everyone, that is…except me. I missed it. My kids were pointing and screaming, "LOOK AT THAT BEAR!" And I kept asking, "WHERE? WHERE?" And for the rest of the trip, they talked about this amazing bear they saw right off the side of the road. It was one of those conversations where everyone has a shared experience, and you're left out of it. This was my opportunity, and I wasn't going to miss it.)

Thank you for listening.

Anyway, as I took out my phone to snap some photos, the bear stopped and turned to look at me. Seriously, we held each other's gaze for more than five seconds (which seemed like much longer). We connected. We had a moment. It was, at the same time, both exhilarating and terrifying.

Then the bear turned around and toddled off, and I breathed a big sigh of relief and continued my run.

Hopefully, you won't run into any physical bears as you go about your day today. But chances are, you'll encounter a few symbolic "bears" at some point in your life.

Moments when you feel afraid and threatened.

Situations where you don't think you have what it takes to move forward.

Experiences that drain you, leaving you depleted of strength.

Circumstances that paralyze you.

Seasons where you want to shrink back and settle for a safe, comfortable life.

I've discovered one of the best responses you can have towards fear is to face it – head-on, fully stare it down. As much as it terrifies you, lock eyes with that "bear". Fear's power over us is diminished when we face it and identify it.

But DON'T LET IT PARALYZE YOU! You must keep running! And if you can't run, walk, and if you can't walk, take a step. Shift your focus to the One who has all power over every fear, over every circumstance, over every "bear", and keep taking steps forward.

God has not turned a deaf ear to your cry for help. No matter how uninterested or uninvolved you may feel God has been in your life, He is very near and longs to comfort and protect you.

Isaiah 41:10 has often been a source of great comfort and peace to me during fearful, anxious, or uncertain times. *"Don't be afraid, for I am with you. Don't be discouraged, for I am your God. I will strengthen you and help you. I will hold you up with my victorious right hand."* Isaiah 41:10 NLT

Throughout this chapter, the phrase from scripture that keeps bubbling up is, *you don't have to be afraid because I am here to help you.*

God doesn't say *fear not* you'll never be hurt by your relationships, or *fear not* you'll never be sick, *fear not* your bank account will always be full, or *fear not* you'll never have pain.

He promises to be with us. He assures us He will help us. We won't have to go through this alone.

When the darkness seems unbearable, when life makes no sense, when fear paralyzes us, God offers us relationship. He offers companionship. He offers to be with us and walk alongside us.

Isn't that a far greater thing?

As much as I try to protect my children, they do get hurt. Scraped knees, bruised elbows, and cutting words occasionally wound them. I can't promise them it won't happen again. But I can promise them a relationship— I can promise to be there for them, care for them, comfort them, and help them through it.

Trust is the foundation for our relationships, so when we limit God by keeping our eyes focused on the "bear", we inadvertently limit our relationship with Him. God wants us to keep running, to continue moving forward.

It's when we encounter fear and, instead of cowering back, we step out, trust Him, and embrace faith, that we truly begin to experience what it is really like to walk by faith and trust in Him. In those moments, we come alive and sense the excitement and fulfillment of the purpose for which He's created us to live.

You don't have to live in the cycle of "what if", "why me", and "if only". Anticipating the unknown and unforeseen wildlife encounters, earthquakes, accidents, hurricanes, heartbreaks, financial problems, or sicknesses will wear you out.

Living in fear won't prevent bad things from happening, but it will prevent us from living the full life God intends for us to experience.

God will comfort, protect, and fill you with His peace to carry you through anything He allows you to experience. Whatever your need or situation, God's grace will be sufficient to face every "bear" and keep moving forward.

Day Four – They're Crazy!

Eight-year-old Jordan was so excited he could hardly wait. He had made a new friend at school and was invited to a sleepover at this boy's house for the first time.

When I picked him up the next day, I asked him how his time was with his new friend.

Jordan quickly shot back, *"They're CRAZY!!!"*

Alarmed, I immediately probed further, "What do you mean? *Are you okay?*"

Jordan reacted bug-eyed, *"Yeah, but they have NO FEAR!"*

Jordan had spent the last 24 hours with a family where both parents were former professional extreme-sport athletes. My little

Jojo had been *charging large* with a family that possessed a thrill for adventure coupled with endless energy!

While Jordan assured me that he had a great time, he added that he was exhausted and relieved to finally be safely buckled into his seat in our minivan.

I often think of that moment and wonder what my life would look like if I were to truly live without fear.

Not the kind fear that brings cautionary restraint, but a confident faith that doesn't hold back and is willing to step into the unknown and risk a little, living with an assurance that God is who He says He is, and He is completely faithful in all He does.

What would I attempt today that I keep making excuses for?

What do I continually put off for tomorrow because I'm a little scared of how it will turn out?

What decision would I make?

What conversations would I have?

What would I say "yes" to?

What would I say "no" to?

How would I work, parent, lead, and love differently if the ominous voice of fear was silenced in my head?

How about you?

It's easy for me to say that I trust God when things are going well. But when things are uncertain, outcomes are unknown, and my life feels like it's turned upside down, to be honest, I doubt. I'm afraid.

Because deep down in my heart, I wonder if God will be good to me. So instead of stepping out…

I grasp for control.

I crave the assurance that everything will be neatly packaged with a cute little bow.

I seek a guarantee that we'll all live happily ever after.

Maybe that's why I love that Jesus doesn't shy away and withdraw from His disciples when they're paralyzed with fear. In fact, in moments of pain, questioning, fear, and doubt, Jesus draws closer to them. In Matthew 8, Jesus and his disciples find themselves in the middle of another storm – the *deadliest catch* kind of storm.

"Then he got into the boat and his disciples followed him. [24] Suddenly a furious storm came up on the lake, so that the waves swept over the boat. But Jesus was sleeping. [25] The disciples went and woke him, saying, 'Lord, save us! We're going to drown!' [26] He replied, 'You of little faith, why are you so afraid?' Then he got up and rebuked the winds and the waves, and it was completely calm. [27] The men were amazed and asked, 'What kind of man is this? Even the winds and the waves obey him!'"
Matthew 8:23-27

Now you'd think Jesus' disciples would've been able to keep it together. They had Jesus in the boat with them! They had seen Jesus perform miracle after miracle – people healed, provision met, and the impossible becoming possible. Yet, even with Him sleeping right next to them, they were afraid.

I get it. If I found myself in a storm out on the open seas in the middle of the night, I would have been right alongside those disciples quaking in my tunic.

Jesus is so kind. He uses this moment to reveal something about Himself. He doesn't take them out of the storm. He doesn't shelter them from experiencing the storm either.

He brings His presence into the storm.

Our source of security is often revealed in the storms of life. It wasn't until the disciples' safety was threatened that their fear and lack of faith was revealed. God doesn't chastise His disciples. He understands how fear can quickly grip our hearts and the tighter grasp of control we'll clasp as a result.

Storms provide an environment for God to do His greatest work within us. In pain, in fear, in difficult and dangerous places, we discover something about ourselves and the powerful presence of God. Throughout the scriptures, God gently reminds us that He is with us and we can trust Him.

One winter, while visiting our parents in Lake Tahoe, a storm quickly rolled in as we drove through the mountain pass. The winds were fierce, the roads were icy, and the snow was beating down on our car.

As my knuckles grew white due to my death grip on my seat, I turned around and saw that my two youngest children were peacefully asleep in their car seats. My heart was quickly convicted as I saw how my babies trusted their earthly daddy to get them home safely, yet how often I fail to fully trust my heavenly Daddy to protect and care for me.

My friend, God is right here with you. You don't walk alone. Don't allow current fear to hinder you from taking a step of courageous faith.

Chart a new course. Create a new path.

For the last several days, I've been pondering this question posed by Erwin McManus as he wrote about living life without regrets, *"Do our feet mark where fear has driven us or where faith has taken us?"*[1]

Where do you need courage today?

What would your life look like if you lived without fear? If your feet marked a new path – one not driven by fear but led by courageous, crazy faith?

Day Five – Puppy Problems

A couple of years ago, we got a new puppy. Might I add, this is *in addition to* the dog and cat we already have in our home of seven grown people.

Possibly a slight lapse in good judgment, but she is really cute. However, when we took her to puppy playtime, we noticed something we hadn't expected from our energetic Ellie. She began to experience social anxiety.

Instead of confidently engaging with the other puppies, our little pup waffled between climbing in Jessie's lap and cowering in the corner.

Sadly, on occasion, I have found that I also have a similar response when I find myself in unfamiliar, uncomfortable situations. Instead of embracing the opportunity of meeting new people and trying new things, I falter and allow the voice of fear to frame my future.

You're not qualified enough.

They won't like you.

What if you fail?

If I'm going to live courageously in this life, I must fight fear every day and cultivate my confidence in God. Unless the truth of God's word defines us and frames our life, something else will.

Let's ask God to help us shift our focus from our fear to the Faithful One. When you sense the voice of fear creeping in, when the grip of anxiety seems to have a chokehold on your life, keep in mind Who your God truly is!

Here are three (of the many) truths I've learned about God to get you started fighting your battle against fear.

God is your Shepherd. You can trust Him to take care of you.

While trust is the foundation of our relationships, it's hard to trust someone we don't know. Trust is developed over time as we grow in relationship with one another.

God wants to know you and desires to have an intimate relationship with you. Your ability to trust God to take care of you will grow as you develop and grow in your relationship with Him.

Psalm 23 describes God as a gentle, nurturing Shepherd who gently leads and guides his flock, watching over them to provide for them and protect them.

In scripture, God often compares us to sheep. Sheep are fearful, vulnerable, and somewhat helpless animals. They can't run very fast and don't have defense mechanisms like sharp teeth or claws to fight off attackers.

They depend heavily on the protection and care of their Shepherd, who enables them to graze peacefully and lie down and get rest. As our heavenly Shepherd, God goes above and beyond—He provides for us and watches over us. His presence creates an environment for us to rest securely, safely, and be refreshed.

Have you ever seen (or perhaps *been*!) a mother whose children wandered into the street? When I sense my children are in danger, I race to protect them.

God loves you with an even greater passion and intensity than a mother possesses toward her children. You can trust Him to be the good and perfect Shepherd who will keep you safe.

God is your Refuge. You are safe with Him.

This scripture tucked in the tiny book Nahum will encourage you to live courageously. *"The Lord is good, a refuge in times of trouble. He cares for those who trust in Him."* Nahum 1:7

A refuge is a place of safety and protection. When fear makes its ugly attempt to creep into my life, and I begin to entertain thoughts questioning God's ability and desire to protect me and keep my family safe, I remind myself that God is good, a refuge in times of trouble.

As I grow in my assurance of God's goodness and His desire to care for me as His daughter, I find my heart growing more at rest and filled with His peace. In His presence, we enter a place of safety and protection.

When trouble hits, when a storm is raging in your life, God offers you a retreat, a safe place, and shelter. He cares for you and will watch over you in times of trouble. God will not forget you. He will be alongside you to walk with you through the storm you are facing.

God surrounds you. You can rest in His presence.

In Psalm 125:1-2, the psalmist uses strong imagery describing God's relationship to his people. "*Those who trust in the LORD are like Mount Zion which cannot be shaken but endures forever. ² As the mountains surround Jerusalem, so the LORD surrounds his people both now and forevermore.*" Psalm 125:1-2

Notice the psalmist didn't choose trees or walls to make his point, but mountains. I can't think of any aspect of God's creation that paints a picture of strength and stability like mountains.

But even more significant than God surrounding us with His mountain-like strength is the truth that as we trust in Him, He places within us the same mountain-like stability (verse 1).

Sometimes I'm able to grasp a concept more fully when I draw a picture of what the author is saying. In the margin, draw a small sketch of verses 1-2 as you envision it.

God surrounds us. And if that isn't enough, He reinforces our life with the strength and stability of the biggest mountains. As we trust Him, there's nothing that can shake or short-circuit the plans God has for our lives. You can live confidently and securely.

During football season, sometimes, we will record our favorite games if we're out for the day. Some members of our family (*eh-hem, I have a confession to make*) like to peek at the final score to know who wins the game before we watch it. It's amazing how relaxed I can be during an intense, nail-biter of a game when I am confident my favorite team will win.

God wants you to be confident knowing He will care for you. You can rest in His presence. Know that He surrounds you and won't allow anything to come into your life that He is not fully prepared to help you walk through.

Learning to trust God, fixing your focus on Him and not on your circumstances, will bring you to a place where God can truly reveal Himself to you. God gives you the opportunity and honor of dwelling in the security, peace, and safety of His presence.

God is your shepherd; you can trust Him.

God is your refuge; He will keep you safe.

And God surrounds you; you can rest in His presence. You don't have to be afraid. He will take care of you.

11

You are Pure

Day One – Purity Matters

If you were given a choice, would you rather drink from a beautiful jewel-studded goblet that was moldy and dirty inside or a simple but squeaky-clean Dixie cup?

I'm going to guess you chose the Dixie cup.

While the goblet may appear beautiful and desirable from the outside, considering its inner grossness, it's not as enticing as the plain, unassuming, but super clean, Dixie cup.

The same is true when it comes to choosing a restaurant. When I eat out, I want to ensure they haven't recently been given a failing grade by the Health Department or by Gordon Ramsay and his undercover crew. If the place is dirty and the food quality is questionable, I'll probably find another restaurant.

The recent Coronavirus pandemic heightened our awareness of germs' dangers and the importance of cleanliness. Hand sanitizers everywhere, disinfectant wipes sold out for months, face masks to accessorize any outfit...in just a matter of days, our senses were heightened and made aware of where germs lurk and the threat they pose to our health.

Why? Because purity matters.

Purity matters to God, too.

In Matthew 5:8, Jesus is teaching His disciples and explaining to them the kind of life that honors God, *"God blesses those whose hearts are pure, for they will see God."* Matthew 5:8 NLT

The Greek word used for *pure* in this verse is *katharos*. It means clean, clear of dirt, spotless and unsoiled.

In her classic book *Passion and Purity*, Elisabeth Elliot defines purity this way: *Purity means freedom from contamination, from anything that would spoil the taste or the pleasure, reduce the power, or in any way adulterate what the thing was meant to be. It means cleanness, clearness—no additives, nothing artificial—in other words, "all-natural", in the sense in which the Original Designer designed it to be.[1]*

I have a habit of spilling food on myself. I rarely make it through a day where I don't wear at least a small portion of one of my meals on my shirt. My husband thinks it's funny; my mom, on occasion, has put stain remover in my Christmas stocking. As for me, well, I think it's just plain embarrassing. I've resolved to always carry a *Tide pen* in my purse.

No matter how hard I wash, scrub, or bleach my clothing, nothing can remove many of my stubborn stains.

Our hearts have been stained by years of sin—wrong attitudes, wrong motives, wrong thinking, wrong relationships, wrong desires. Just as no amount of my human strength can remove my clothing stains, no amount of human effort can change the condition of our hearts.

We can attempt to give the appearance of having a neat, clean life. We can compare ourselves to those around us, hoping to find someone worse than we are. We can judge and criticize others to feel better about our inadequacies. We can mask our flaws and comfort ourselves, thinking nobody sees our weaknesses.

But how do you live when no one else is around?

How's *your* heart?

The writer of Proverbs was serious in his challenge when he wrote, *"Above all else, guard your heart, for everything you do flows from it."* Proverbs 4:23

Notice we're not asked to "follow our heart". Instead, we're instructed *to guard our hearts*. What does that mean?

I'm glad you asked.

Your heart, in this verse, speaks of the deepest part of your being. It's not the beating, blood-pumping organ. It's your soul.

The instruction to *guard our hearts* reminds us of our responsibility to actively watch over what goes into our hearts and what comes out. This isn't a casual activity. It's not something we can passively ignore; it isn't something that happens naturally. We must do the consistent, diligent work of tending our hearts.

Think of your heart as a reservoir, a pool of water that is your main source of life. If the water is contaminated, stagnant, and filled with impurities, all the streams flowing from it will also be impure. You could work hard to clean each stream, but the streams will continue to be infected if the reservoir is polluted.

American philosopher, Dallas Willard, described it this way, *"Our soul is like a stream of water, which gives strength, direction, and harmony to every other area of our life. When that stream is as it should be, we are constantly refreshed and exuberant in all we do, because our soul itself is then profusely rooted in the vastness of God and his kingdom, including nature; and all else within us is enlivened and directed by that stream. Therefore we are in harmony with God, reality, and the rest of human nature and nature at large."*[2]

Wow! That's a lot. Let's consider this a bit further. If all your thoughts, attitudes, and choices you make flow from the condition of your heart, it makes sense that we give great care and concern to its condition. Unfortunately, we tend to invest more energy and focus on other areas. A new haircut, cute outfit, trendy color lipstick, or stylish shoes may give us a quick emotional boost but won't give us long-term heart health. It's merely beautifying the outside of the "cup" while leaving the dirtiness of the inside unattended.

I used to think that purity was something *I* was responsible for doing. I had to clean up my life, attitudes, words, thoughts, and actions. The trouble was that I could never *do enough,* and I constantly fell short and, as a result, felt extremely inadequate, full of shame, and a failure.

While we do have a part to play regarding the care and condition of our hearts, the Good News of Jesus is that He is the ultimate, all-powerful purifier. The Old Testament prophet Malachi even refers to the coming Messiah as someone who will be like a refiner's fire and launderer's soap (Malachi 3:2).

This means that we don't have to do the work of purifying our hearts. Jesus does that. Our job is to guard our hearts. To protect it, care for it, watch over it, and be concerned about its health because everything we do flows from it.

Day Two – What's that Smell?

We had just finished a week-long, cross-country move from Austin to San Diego with our growing family of four. (You're possibly a little confused, *"Don't they live in Hawaii...or was it Nashville...or maybe LA?"* Quick summary: Los Angeles to Hawaii to Orange County to Austin to San Diego to Los Angeles to Nashville to Hawaii. Yes, many, many boxes, many, many moves.)

Typical moving aftermath, boxes, and packing paper were scattered everywhere throughout our home when we woke to an oppressively pungent odor. This aroma was quite possibly the WORST smell I've ever encountered – think part death, part rotten eggs. It was *THAT BAD.*

I opened the windows hoping that the smell would dissipate by airing out the home, but it only grew stronger and more nauseating. The stench eventually led us to our driveway, where we discovered ground zero.

A skunk had been hit by a car and conveniently crawled to its death in our driveway. Nothing says, "Welcome to the neighborhood!" quite like that.

In 2 Corinthians 2, Paul describes the effect the Corinthian Christians' lives had on those around them. *"But thanks be to God, who always leads us as captives in Christ's triumphal procession and uses us to spread the aroma of the knowledge of him everywhere.* [15] *For we are to God the pleasing aroma of Christ among those who are being saved and those who are perishing.* [16] *To the one we are an aroma that brings death; to the*

other, an aroma that brings life. And who is equal to such a task?"
2 Corinthians 2:14-16

There's a lot of research revealing how different aromas can affect our brains and emotions. Paul uses something as tangible as the smell in the air to illustrate the potent affect our lives can have on others. God works through us to spread the aroma of the knowledge of Him everywhere!

To some, our lives will be a sweet fragrant perfume. They will see our lives and desire to know more about the God we serve. To others, our lives may be received with the aroma of a stinky dead skunk. They don't want anything to do with it.

But there's something else to consider. The sobering reality is that we can stink up the air by how we live and represent Christ.

The big question is, *"What 'scent' am I diffusing?"*

I want to do my part to represent Christ honorably, making Him attractive to others instead of repelling people by the things I say and how I live.

There are enough barriers, excuses, and reasons why people choose not to follow Christ. I don't want to add another one.

One of the primary ways our culture and community will be drawn to Christ is through the lifestyle and behavior of His followers. For us to accurately represent Christ, we should make it our goal to please Him and be like Him as much as possible.

Peter describes it this way. He's addressing the Christians in the region of Galatia who, as young believers, were feeling like foreigners in their hometown. *"So you must live as God's obedient children. Don't slip back into your old ways of living to satisfy your own desires. You didn't know any better then. ¹⁵But now you must be holy in everything you do, just as God who chose you is holy. ¹⁶For the Scriptures say, 'You must be holy because I am holy.'"* 1 Peter 1:14-16 NLT

Your life is part of a bigger story. God is at work, and He has invited you to be an important part of showing Himself to the world! Purity isn't just about obeying a bunch of rules and trying to stay out of sin. He wants to make you more like Jesus so your life will display God's love and glory to a broken world.

When others spend time with you, they should smell the scent of God's presence at work in your life like a sweet aroma.

Because we have two dogs and a cat, sometimes I try to cover up the animal smell by spraying air freshener. While it works temporarily, it doesn't fix the problem. The animal smell is still there; I've only covered the problem.

God doesn't want us to mask or filter our behavior; He wants to change our hearts. In Jesus, you are pure, holy, and righteous before God. The stench of sin is removed, and you can now diffuse the sweet fragrant aroma representing the love and purity of Christ.

Day Three – You Can Cry Now

When we were starting our family and living in Austin, Gregg and I had the exciting opportunity to buy and build a home.

Our first home. A new home. *Brand new.* (Remember our faulty foundation from Chapter Two?)

With the paint on the walls barely dry, we began to feel God's tugging on our hearts once again. We'd felt that tug before. It was God beginning to pull us towards something new.

Just months after moving into this cute little starter home in the Austin suburbs, we sold it, packed up, moved back to the West coast, and rented a house in San Diego.

Keep in mind this was long ago, back in the ancient days, when your phone was attached to a wall in your house and didn't come with a 12-megapixel camera. The internet was "dial-up", and you still had to use the Classified Ads in a *PAPER NEWSPAPER* to find a rental home.

We had yet to see our rental in our new city, but from everything the owner described, it *sounded* beautiful. Large double doors, huge backyard, newly renovated bathrooms, ceramic tile flooring throughout most of the house…

We *thought* we had scored.

After the long cross-country drive, as we pulled into the driveway with hopeful anticipation, Gregg immediately turned to me and said, *"It's ok. You can cry now."*

He proceeded to drive me straight to the nearest Starbucks for comfort and consolation because nothing communicates *"I care"* better than a sugary, caffeinated coffee drink.

This home that *sounded* so good was the eyesore of the neighborhood. Overgrown yard, peeling paint on the house's exterior, old pink countertops in the kitchen, worn carpet – it was quite *"something"*. (By the way, this is the same home that surprised us with a stinky dead skunk as a housewarming gift.)

As much as I wanted to have a good attitude about the whole thing, I didn't. I dreamt of newer carpets and freshly sodded yards.

And I complained – a lot.

It's been said that when we complain, we're calling into question God's provision for us. In our frustration, we're expressing that what God is giving us isn't good enough.[3]

We're inadvertently saying that we deserve *more*.

That we're entitled to something *better*.

Ouch.

How often do I find myself drifting into this attitude every day? Even with the small stuff. The weather, the traffic, the laundry, the kids, the dogs, the cat, the house, my job…

I'm really skilled at finding things to complain about.

Perhaps this is why Paul sternly warned the Philippian people about the slippery slope of our complaining. He advised, *"Do everything without grumbling or arguing,* [15] *so that you may become blameless and pure, 'children of God without fault in a warped and crooked generation.' Then you will shine among them like stars in the sky...*" Philippians 2:14-15

The last time I looked, *everything* meant *every* thing. All that exists. What would my life look like if I refused to grumble about everything?

What would your life look like if you refused to complain?

How might our attitude change if we considered God the unintentional target of our frustration?

Paul, in his writing, often encourages the recipients to do "something", *so that* "something else" will result. Paul tells the Christ-followers in Philippi to *do everything without grumbling or arguing* – so that – *they may become blameless and pure...*

When we make a choice to shift our focus from grumbling to gratitude, something marvelous occurs. God works in us, making us blameless and pure in His sight.

When we intentionally shift our focus from what we lack and think we deserve to the lavish provision of God's love and His undeserved grace toward us, the grip of selfishness begins to break.

Even more importantly, when you choose to be grateful for what God has given you, your life will shine brightly. You'll stand out from the crowd of cantankerous complainers.

Pastor Craig Groeschel explains it this way, "If you can't change your circumstances, change your perspective."[4]

God will be glorified as you shift your focus from your frustration to His gracious provision. Others will be drawn to the life you have, and you will shine like stars in the sky!

We can always find something to complain about. Let's practice thanking God for all His blessings – even if they're pink kitchen countertops.

Day Four – An Everyday Offering

One Christmas, Gregg presented me with a beautifully wrapped gift. Upon removing the wrapping paper, I discovered a cell phone box! Elated, I started thanking him profusely because I didn't have a mobile phone.

He immediately began to offer a lot of disclaimers, such as, *"Don't get tooooo enthusiastic yet." "It's not that big of a gift."*

I was confused…until I realized Gregg had used the box from the recent purchase of *his* cell phone to disguise a gift for *me*.

What he gave me: a *Switchfoot* CD. Not that there's anything wrong with *Switchfoot*. As much as I enjoy their music, I wasn't expecting a CD. I was expecting a cell phone.

I proceeded to educate him on the proper rules of *gift-wrapping etiquette*. The main point: don't wrap a "lesser gift" in a more desirable gift box.

When God gave us Jesus as a sacrifice for our sins, He gave us the most incredible gift. He held nothing back.

Jesus humbly arrived wrapped in flesh – so unassuming that many missed His arrival. They were anticipating all the bells and bows of a powerful king, but Jesus came with the care and compassion of a simple carpenter.

Jesus asks us to lead and love others in the same pattern He demonstrated for us – with simple humility and holiness in how we live. We get the best gift ever. Honoring Him in the way we live and living a life worthy of the sacrifice He made are ways we can thank God for His generous gift every day.

If someone saved your life, I'm guessing you'd be super grateful. You'd honor them by living with purpose and intention because they gave you the precious gift of life. You'd have a reverence and respect for them and would most likely go to great lengths if they requested something from you. You wouldn't receive their request as a burden because they had done so much for you.

Paul explains this idea to the Christians in Rome, "*So here's what I want you to do, God helping you: Take your everyday, ordinary life—your sleeping, eating, going-to-work, and walking-around life—and place it before God as an offering. Embracing what God does for you is the best thing you can do for him. Don't become so well-adjusted to your culture that you fit into it without even thinking. Instead, fix your attention on God. You'll be changed from the inside out."* Romans 12:1 MSG

When the New Testament was written, the Bible, as we know it, didn't exist. People were attracted to Christianity because of what they saw and heard in the lives of those around them. The lifestyle of the early Christians was different from the cultural norm in which they lived – not irrelevant or unrelatable – but different, and people were attracted to it.

When we honor God with how we live, others become aware of His grace and goodness. Jesus offered the way to a holy and pure life, not by forcing us to clean our lives up, not by requiring us to be perfect, and not by prohibiting failure or making mistakes. His path to purity for us is through the cross.

He became unclean so we could become clean. Jesus provided for us what we were completely helpless to accomplish by ourselves. He died for us. Through His death and resurrection, our sins are taken away, and we can enjoy the intimate relationship with God that we were created to have. We can live a pure life that is holy and pleasing to God because He loves us so much.

It has absolutely nothing to do with what we have or haven't done. All the filth, all the shame, all the guilt, and all our sin, Christ takes away. He cleanses, restores, and makes us useful for His purpose once again. You don't have to drag yourself around in filthy clothes. You don't have to clean yourself up. You don't have

to hide. You are pure and holy in His sight. And that's the best gift
ever.

Day Five – Beauty in Brokenness

With the anticipated arrival of our third child, we entered full-family mode and purchased a minivan. After seven years of having one car, I was excited to have a second car. I protected it like it was one of my kids – kept it clean (as much as you can with two toddlers) and parked in the weeds at every shopping center.

One evening, an unexpected thing occurred while unloading the groceries from the back of my brand-new, sparkly clean car.

(What happened next, I blame on a combination of being eight months pregnant and the sheer exhaustion from a long day of parenting toddlers.)

Pulling the car into the garage, I heard a thud...followed by a crack...followed by a loud crash!

Apparently, I forgot to close the rear liftgate. (Helpful hint, most minivans do not fit through a standard garage opening with the rear liftgate open.) My brand-new, sparkly-clean minivan now had a crippled, cracked, and crinkly backend.

As we journey through life, we will be dinged, dented, and occasionally damaged. Whether it's choices we've made, things we've done, or things that have been done to us, our natural response is often to hide our hurts and believe the lie that because of our past, God can't use us.

Regardless of how many times you've failed or fallen short, you're not damaged goods. You're not an embarrassment or burden to God. He doesn't discard broken things…He restores them.

Kintsugi is the ancient style of Japanese art used to repair broken pottery. Translated, it means "golden joinery". This unique method uses a special lacquer dusted with powdered gold, silver, or platinum to restore the broken ceramic piece. Instead of hiding the fracture with a transparent adhesive, the *Kintsugi* method illuminates the brokenness highlighting it with beautiful streams of precious metal that flow through the cracks. *Kintsugi* treats breakage and repair as part of the history of an object instead of something to disguise.[5]

Many might argue that the original piece is more beautiful *after* the repair than *before* the damage because the precious metal beautifully illuminates the brokenness and graces the pottery with unique beauty.

Doesn't this reflect God's work in our life? He takes the cracks, fractures, and broken pieces of our lives and illuminates them to make something beautiful. You don't have to hide or cover them – just allow Him to work through them.

King David understood this. In 2 Samuel 11, we read how he had messed up big time. In a season of weakness and spiritual complacency, David had an affair with another man's wife, who became pregnant. And if that wasn't enough, he attempted to cover up his sin by having the husband killed.

When we mess up, aren't we tempted to hide and cover our sins too? But God is so merciful.

David experienced God's grace firsthand. Psalm 51 is a song of repentance David wrote during this intense season of brokenness. David cries out to God for compassion and forgiveness revealing his desperation to honor God once again. His precious plea should be the cry of our hearts as well.

David prays, *"Create in me a pure heart, O God, and renew a steadfast spirit within me. [11] Do not cast me from your presence or take your Holy Spirit from me. [12] Restore to me the joy of your salvation and grant me a willing spirit, to sustain me."* Psalm 51:10-12

David wasn't asking for a Bible teaching or a formula to feel better. He wanted God – His presence and friendship. The cry of David's heart was for a relationship with the living God. He desired to honor and glorify God. He craved an intimate relationship that surpassed his other relationships.

David's cry revealed a tender heart that was hungry for the presence of God once again. David sought not only to be pure but also to dwell in God's presence. He didn't strive for outward righteousness by keeping a list of rules. It was the love and intimacy that David had toward God that motivated him to live a pure life.

But David also knew that on his own effort, he could never be made pure in God's sight. Only God could purify his heart.

Through the shed blood of Jesus on the cross, Jesus offered the way to a holy and pure life, not by forcing us to strive to clean ourselves up or by requiring us to be perfect and not make mistakes.

The writer of Hebrews said it this way, *"Just think how much more the blood of Christ will purify our consciences from sinful deeds so that we can worship the living God. For by the power of the eternal Spirit, Christ offered himself to God as a perfect sacrifice for our sins."* Hebrews 9:14 NLT

Regardless of where your past has taken you, you no longer have to be ashamed. You don't have to live your life weighed down by guilt or insecurity.

Invite the blood of Christ to wash away your sins and purify your heart. As you pursue God and His presence, your trust in Him will grow, you'll walk closer with Him, and He will restore you from the inside out. He is the Master *Kintsugi* artist.

12

You are Never Alone

Day One – Created for Community

During a season of planning and preparing for a big move to a new city, I was physically and emotionally exhausted. In tears and with the defiance of a three-year-old, I begged Gregg, *"I don't want to make friends again!"*

Nothing magnifies the connection we were created to crave, like packing your entire life into cardboard boxes, saying tearful goodbyes to tons of people, and moving thousands of miles away.

At the time, the fear and uncertainty paralyzed me. Everything in me wanted to stay in the safety net of my familiar friendships. I didn't want to put forth the effort to build relationships again. I'd worked hard for my friendships and didn't want to let go of them. (Cue: stomp of foot and dig in heels here.)

Yet, my longing for relationships and my growing awareness of my need for other women in my life motivates me time and time again to break through the awkwardness and shallow pleasantries to journey deeper in life with other people.

God is so faithful because the new friendships I made—while they didn't replace the old ones—became just as valued and cherished over time. But, had I hibernated, erected walls, and stayed in my cave of self-pity, I wouldn't have enjoyed the blessing, wisdom, and encouragement these friendships continue to provide year after year.

God never intended us to live this life alone. He created us with an inherent need and desire to connect with Him and with others. Built within the core of who we are is a need—not for crowds—but for community.

You may try to suppress it, deny it, avoid it, or make excuses for it, but deep down in your heart, there exists a need for intimacy – shared first and foremost with God and then also to be experienced with others.

Genesis 1 broadly describes God's creation of the world. As the Master Artist is busy creating, after each masterpiece, there is this declaration: *"And God saw that it was good."* (See Genesis 1:4, 9, 12, 18, 21, 27, 31)

But as we read on to Genesis 2, we notice a startling reversal, *"The LORD God said, 'It is not good for the man to be alone. I will make a helper suitable for him.'"* Genesis 2:18

Adam enjoyed complete intimacy and communion with God, yet God describes his "aloneness" as "not good". I don't think this statement implies that God is not enough or that He is insufficient to fulfill our lives. However, it does reveal that we fully enjoy the beauty and richness of God's creation as we experience relationship with one another.

You were created for community. Community nourishes our souls and frees us to flourish. We all need people who will...

Stand with us.

Support us.

Encourage us.

Celebrate with us.

Cry with us.

Speak truth to us.

Pray with us.

And maybe even challenge us from time to time.

Our effectiveness in what God has called us to do increases when we lock arms in community with others. The Scriptures reveal that while we have a personal relationship with God, our calling and purpose flourish in community.

It's community that sustains us no matter how many times we move, how many of our friends leave, and how many changes and transitions we experience.

God can always widen our circle, provide life-giving community, and grow our faith when we make an effort to plant ourselves in His kingdom and connect with others.

Day Two – The Costa Rican Family Reunion

Years ago, Gregg's Costa Rican grandma (Abuela) decided to throw a big party. She went all out – rented a ballroom in a hotel, served a delicious buffet, and flew in her relatives from Costa Rica. (Abuela was one of thirteen children, so this was no small shindig.)

We worked out the babysitting responsibilities with Gregg's sister, Cherie. Cherie and her husband took the first shift and stayed in our hotel room with the kids, while Gregg and I went to the party with three-month-old Justin.

We took a seat at our table, got our stroller and baby gear situated in the crowded ballroom (no small feat), and settled in for dinner. Spanish flowed, paella was served, and Latin music abounded. Not wanting to neglect our duties with the older kids, Gregg went to check on them and said, *"I'll be right back."*

Only he didn't come back.

I waited.

And waited.

And waited with my fussy newborn while awkwardly nodding and smiling as the beautiful Spanish language streamed from extended relatives who were most likely trying to figure out who I was and why I was at their party.

With every passing minute, I grew more and more frustrated. *How long does it take to check on our kids and come back?!*

After what seemed like an eternity but was only about 40 minutes, I packed up the massive quantity of equipment moms with newborns travel with and went searching for my husband. (This was in the pre-historic, pre-cell phone, pre-text messaging times. You had to track someone down IN PERSON to find them. *Hardships*.)

As I neared the door of our hotel room, the booming sounds of laughter, children's voices, and activity echoed into the hall.

Apparently, the party had moved, and I didn't get the invite.

Gregg, our kids, and his sister's family were having so much fun in the hotel room that they lost track of time and didn't come back to get me.

And that is how I found myself alone at the Costa Rican family reunion. Well, technically, I wasn't *all alone*. People were all around me. But I felt that way.

How can we live in big cities, work in large offices, be surrounded by people, and fill our social schedules with lunch and coffee appointments, yet still sometimes feel painfully alone?

Even though I had Justin with me, the awkwardness of not feeling like I belonged was unsettling and uncomfortable.

We all will feel this way on occasion. You have a real and legitimate need to feel like you belong, are loved, and are valued.

Many of us, though, find loneliness tugging us into a deep dark hole of despair, isolation, and sometimes depression. Social anxiety chokes us … loneliness cloaks us in darkness…

Like quicksand, the harder we fight, the deeper we go, and the more overwhelmed we become.

If you are struggling with feelings of hopelessness or depression, I urge you to talk to someone and get help. It is a slow, fierce battle that should not be fought alone, and it's all right to ask for help from a trusted friend, small group leader, or counselor.

In Genesis 16, we read about Hagar, a woman who knew what it was like to feel the despair of being alone and abandoned.

As a servant to Sarai, Hagar found herself in a tough situation. God promised Sarai's husband, Abram, that he would have descendants as numerous as the stars in the sky. But Sarai had not borne any children. With every year, her biological clock ticking, she despaired that she was the one hindering the fulfillment of God's promise to her husband.

In her impatience, Sarai gave Hagar to her husband, hoping that she could have a family through her. Believe it or not, this was an acceptable thing to do in their culture.[1] (Spoiler alert: even though culturally acceptable, if you give your servant to your husband for the purpose of conceiving a child, you're probably going to have some problems.)

The conception of a baby in Hagar's womb birthed jealousy and resentment towards Hagar in Sarai's heart. Almost instantly, their relationship turned tense and toxic.

Jealous stares. Condemning comments. Harsh glares. Critical remarks. Sarai treated Hagar so harshly that finally, Hagar couldn't take it anymore and ran away.

Hagar must have felt so alone – unloved, used, betrayed. Pregnant and alone in the desert, God didn't forget her. He didn't leave her alone. He sent an angel to comfort her and be with her.

When the angel of the Lord appears to Hagar, she gives the Lord the name *El Roi*, the God Who Sees. "*She gave this name to the LORD who spoke to her: 'You are the God who sees me,' for she said, 'I have now seen the One who sees me.'*" Genesis 16:13

You are the God Who Sees.

You are the God Who Sees *me*.

When I hurt.

When I cry.

When I suffer.

When I feel all alone.

You are the God Who Sees me.

Hagar, a woman who had been betrayed, abandoned, left alone, and discarded.

He is the *God Who Sees*.

What a beautiful promise for us.

Another name for God in the Old Testament is *Immanuel* (Isaiah 7:14), meaning *God with us*. God sees you, and He is with you. God notices every detail of your life. Even when you're feeling unappreciated and unnoticed, God sees your life when nobody else does.

He knows when you're weary and when you feel all alone.

Not only does He see you. He is *with you* in your pain. The Creator of the universe sees YOU and promises to be with YOU!

He is *El Roi*, the God Who Sees…you.

Day 3 – The New Girl

With every move we've made, I've had to decide how I will respond: *Will I wilt and wallow in self-pity, or will I choose to bloom where I am planted?*

Thankfully, my bouts of pouting are usually short-lived, and I eventually choose the latter. But one thing I've noticed about being the *new girl*.

The phone doesn't ring that often.

The invitations to lunch, coffee, and playdates with the kids – are few and far between.

It's hard to be the new girl on campus.

The new mom at school.

The new woman in the office.

The new family in the neighborhood.

People have busy schedules and already have close-knit groups of friends. It can be awkward to find your place as an unfamiliar person in everyone else's familiar world.

Whether you're the newbie or not, we will all experience seasons when we feel lonely, like an outsider, or perhaps distant and disconnected relationally. We were created for community, and when we're not experiencing a relational connection with others, we can feel so alone.

Maybe that's why I appreciate the honesty King David expresses to God regarding the loneliness and isolation he felt, "*I look for someone to come and help me, but no one gives me a passing thought! No one will help me; no one cares a bit what happens to me.*" Psalm 142:4 NLT

Sometimes, we feel like that, don't we? Unappreciated. Uninvited. Unloved. Uncared for.

But in the words of *Winnie the Pooh* himself, *"You can't stay in your corner of the Forest waiting for others to come to you. You have to go to them sometimes."* [2]

Too often, we don't initiate a friendship with others because we're waiting for them to come to us. And then we're disappointed when we're not invited to a get-together or included in a conversation.

We can make excuses and wait for the phone to ring or the text invite to come. We can blame others who don't make an effort to include us or reach out to us.

Pooh's words challenge us to take responsibility for our social life by taking the first step to building a friendship. If you're lonely, take a step and make an invite.

In every new environment, I've had to step out of the sadness of missing my old friends to step into a season of building new friendships. I encourage you to do the same.

Trust me. If you're waiting for the phone to ring or the text to magically come, you'll probably be waiting a long time. Even worse, you're missing out on the life-giving relationships God has for you in this new season!

So, where do you start?

First, take the initiative. Don't wait for people to call you. Invite another mom to the park for a playdate. Ask someone in your class to study with you. Join a small group with other women at your church. Invite your neighbor out for coffee.

Instead of becoming jealous of everyone's Instagram photos highlighting the fun they're having with friends at the beach, eating out, and celebrating sports events and birthdays, create your own pockets of new friendships.

Second, take your time. Relationships take time to build. I remember one season when our kids were little – in addition to being in a new city – we only had one car. It was a lot of work just to get out of the house! But there was a McDonald's with a play area within walking distance from our house. I decided that I would invite other moms to meet me there every week with their littles.

Gradually, week by week, friendships were built over Happy Meals. They didn't replace the dear friends I had left, but they helped fill the void of loneliness I had been experiencing. And guess what? They were feeling alone and isolated too!

Lastly, don't give up. You're not going to be BFFs with everyone. But you'll never know who a potential friend for you may be if you choose to *stay in your corner of the forest.* Don't let fear keep you locked in isolation.

We're better when we're together. The writer of Hebrews explained it this way, *"And let us consider how we may spur one another on toward love and good deeds, ²⁵ not giving up meeting together, as some are in the habit of doing, but encouraging one another—and all the more as you see the Day approaching."* Hebrews 10:24-25

Don't give up. Venture out of the corner of your forest to allow new friendships to breathe life into your weary soul. It's in the community of friendships where we bloom and become the women God created us to be.

Day Four – Refresh the Weary

Our lives are hectic, and our planners are full. We have the amazing ability to cram more activity into a day only to discover that at the end of the day, instead of feeling a sense of accomplishment, we're empty and depleted.

We're more "connected" than ever. We have more access to information. We have apps and devices to work more, connect more, and accomplish more. But research reveals we're more tired and overwhelmed than ever.

We're also more anxious and lonelier than ever. This may be the reason Great Britain saw the necessity to appoint an official Minister of Loneliness.[3] Amid the recent COVID crisis, Japan has followed suit in efforts to combat its rising suicide rates.

With smartphones and social media accounts pinging nonstop, our attention is constantly alerted to what we're missing out on and not measuring up to. Add all this activity to your work demands, family commitments, and the basics of taking care of yourself, it's easy to end your day feeling empty and overwhelmed.

Only to start it all again the next day. *sigh*

When you're giving so much throughout the day, how do you begin to find your way out of the empty place? Where do you go to fill your thirsty soul?

Throughout the Gospels, Jesus guides us to a place where we can refresh our weary souls.

"Yet the news about him spread all the more, so that crowds of people came to hear him and to be healed of their sicknesses. [16] But Jesus often withdrew to lonely places and prayed." Luke 5:15-16

Jesus had crowds of people around Him constantly! Everywhere Jesus went, He was met with expectations, demands, assumptions, and needs. I tire just thinking about the weight of responsibility He carried.

Yet, in the chaos of the crowds, He chose to withdraw to spend time with His Father.

I have found that God will often use seasons when I'm feeling empty, overwhelmed, or lonely as an opportunity to draw me closer to Him.

To quiet the noise.

To pause the activity.

To stop being productive.

To spend time with God.

It can be so hard to do – especially when the demands for time and attention are nonstop. I like accomplishing things. I enjoy crossing things off my "to-do" list. Sitting and spending time with Jesus seems counter-intuitive.

But don't let that fool you! To breathe life into your weary soul, you must create space in your crammed schedule.

Think about it. Relationships are built in the margins of life. You can't rush a relationship, squeezing it into the ten minutes you have between your children's soccer practice and dance class.

Yet that's what we try to do with Jesus. Our relationship with Him is reduced to "breakfast on the run". You grab your coffee, a Clif bar, and a Bible scripture as you run out the door.

To fill our thirsty souls, we must drink deeply. This implies sitting still long enough. I'm known for spilling coffee on myself. Most of the time, this happens because I'm trying to "walk and sip" and "do and drink" instead of sitting down and enjoying it.

Jesus continually invites us to experience the depth of relationship with Him that He enjoys with the Father. In John 7, He gives an invitation during one of the annual Jewish feasts, the *Feast of Booths*. In observance of the festival, the Israelites camped for seven days, ending with a huge feast. Think Thanksgiving dinner without Costco or your kitchen (no pressure).

The *Feast of Booths* was one week of the year when God commanded the Jewish people to cease their work to rest and reflect on God's goodness. It was intentional time set aside to recalibrate their souls.

An important theme throughout the feast was water. Jerusalem is situated in a desert climate, so water was essential for them to thrive. During the seven days, they prayed earnestly for rain and even held a water ceremony where the priest would draw water from the pool of Siloam and pour it into the basin near the altar in the temple. [4]

In John 7, Jesus stands before the people on the greatest day of the festival and gives this invitation... *"On the last and most important day of the festival Jesus stood up and said in a loud voice, 'Whoever is thirsty should come to me, and [38] whoever believes in me should drink. As the scripture says, 'Streams of life-giving water will pour out from his side.'"* John 7:37-38

Jesus is brilliant! He uses water to illustrate the satisfaction He has to offer them. He does this at a feast where they pray for abundant rain and celebrate God's goodness. He references a scripture from the Old Testament book of Isaiah that would have been familiar to them.

Jesus boldly calls people to Himself, claiming He can satisfy our inner thirst. He shouts out His invitation to anyone who wants to have the water of life bubbling up inside them and flowing out to the world.

The people listening knew that water was vital to their livelihood and symbolic of spiritual refreshment – God's refreshing personal presence.

Jesus' invitation to come to Him is an invitation to come to the only One who can truly save and satisfy our thirsty souls. Jesus is present. Ready to fill.

But you must come.

You must break away from the busy to sit in His presence. It's in His presence where He refreshes, restores, and provides a quiet place of rest and refuge.

By coming to Him every day, asking Jesus to fill you with His presence, and spending time with Him by reading the Bible and prayer, you will discover streams of living water begin to bubble up inside of you. Instead of being overwhelmed and empty, you'll be overflowing with the refreshing, restful presence of Jesus.

Day Five – Be a Blessing

There have been days when I have felt alone in my responsibilities of motherhood. The endless laundry, piles of dishes, sports practices, homework, and other needs, can drain me and sometimes overwhelm me.

It's usually about this time when the faint sound of violins begins to play, and I start to whine my sad song to myself that my husband quietly comes in, does the dishes, folds the laundry, and reminds me I'm not in this alone. While Gregg helps me a lot and does his part to keep our home running, sometimes we moms can feel underappreciated and underwater with all the daily responsibilities. Can I get an *"Amen"*?

In Exodus 17:8-16, we read about an event that occurred while the Israelites were waiting to enter the Promised Land. A band of Amalekite warriors attacked the Israelites. Moses, the leader of the

Israelites, told Joshua to choose some men to go with them to battle. During the battle, the Jewish community noticed something strange happening. The Israelites won while Moses held his staff in the air. But whenever he lowered his arms, Joshua and the Israelite army would begin to lose the fight.

That's when Aaron and Hur (Moses' brother and friend, respectively) surrounded and supported him. When Moses grew weary, they held up his hands for him. Scripture doesn't tell us if Moses asked them to do this. They just showed up.

That's the beautiful part of having a community. When we're weary, our people show up to rally around us and hold us up. And when others are struggling, we're there to hold them up.

No one should ever have to walk alone. Throughout scripture, we see how God desires to bless us to be a blessing to others (Genesis 12:1-2).

I'm embarrassed to admit it, but sometimes my focus is more on *being blessed* than it is on *being a blessing*. My attention can quickly become myopic and self-centered.

God didn't create us that way. When sin entered in Genesis 3, the devotion of our hearts shifted from focusing on the *kingdom of God* to focus on *being the king of our own kingdom*. We may not throw a tantrum in Target like our toddler, but our hearts are still selfish. Our selfishness just looks a little different. It's packaged a little neater.

We're good at masking it, and most people won't even see it – until someone's need infringes on the boundary of our kingdom.

When we don't get our way on the work project, we give everyone on the team the silent treatment.

We make up creative reasons to be excused from the responsibility of helping at our kids' school.

Or possibly, we snap at our family when someone takes the last piece of our secret chocolate stack. Confession…Guilty…That would be me.

Selfish hearts reign when we're the king of our own kingdom.

This seemed to be an issue in the Philippian church too. In Philippians 4:2, Paul boldly calls out Euodia and Syntyche on their bickering, urging them to live in harmony with one another. (How would you like to be forever remembered for that? Yikes!)

This rebuke follows his encouragement to the entire Philippian church to consider their actions and the motives of their hearts. *"Don't be selfish; don't try to impress others. Be humble, thinking of others as better than yourselves. ⁴ Don't look out only for your own interests, but take an interest in others, too."* Philippians 2:3-4 NLT

We all know it's the right thing to do. But it's… so… incredibly… hard to do. Maybe that's why Paul swiftly followed these verses with a command, *"You must have the same attitude that Christ Jesus had."* Philippians 2:5

Paul doesn't suggest this or recommend this; he commands it. Paul knows the danger of a selfish heart. When we're the king of our own kingdom, we want to do the things we want, when we want, and the way we want. Instead of serving others, we try to impress them.

That's why Paul follows this instruction by unveiling the secret weapon to crippling selfishness.

Humility.

It's been said that humility isn't thinking less of yourself. It's thinking of yourself less. It's allowing yourself to be inconvenienced by the needs and concerns of others. Jesus modeled this for us when He willingly laid down His life to pay the price for our sins. Jesus didn't become any *less* than God when He died on the cross. His humility was modeled by laying aside His power and authority to serve us.

God didn't run away from you—He ran to you. In a world filled with selfishness, He sought and served you, making a way for you to experience a relationship with Him.

He now asks us to do the same for others.

Back to Exodus 17… Aaron and Hur probably had a lot going on that day. They were in the middle of a battle, and as leaders in the community of Israel, there were decisions to make and things to do. But they set aside their own agendas to serve their friend. They showed up and stayed all day.

Most likely, you have a lot going on today as well. Who needs you? Whose arms are weary and could use a little energy boost to get them through the day?

Choose to be a blessing to someone today. Use your secret weapon of humility to drive selfishness out of your heart so Christ can shine brightly in a broken world.

13

You are Free

Day One – Thanksgiving Turkey Troubles

Thanksgiving is one of my favorite holidays. It's a day to reflect on God's goodness, enjoy the special relationships in our lives, and celebrate God's continued faithfulness. It's a day to watch football games and parades, eat an excessive amount of food, and create a wonderful meal for my favorite people.

While I'm no *Pioneer Woman*, I enjoy investing a lot of thought and time into preparing our Thanksgiving feast. A few weeks before the big day, I begin looking through my cookbooks, gathering my favorite recipes, compiling the grocery list, and developing a master plan of execution for the preparation of the many dishes that vie for prime oven space.

One Thanksgiving several years ago, as the smell of turkey wafted in the air, Jessie and I sat down to catch a few minutes of the parade while Gregg and the boys headed to the beach for a quick surf session.

Before engrossing myself in the holiday floats, high school marching bands, and the Radio City Rockettes, I thought I'd better check on my turkey and baste it one more time. However, as I attempted to open the oven door, it wouldn't open. The door was stuck, trapping my turkey inside!

Seriously, the door would only open about six inches. Somehow, the latch at the base of the oven door had broken and wedged itself in the most peculiar place, jamming the door and preventing it from opening.

We tried EVERYTHING!

Pounding it.

Prying it.

Shaking it.

Kicking it.

Face-timing family members for advice.

Nothing worked.

So there my turkey sat, in my oven, fully cooked (I hoped), with no way of escape.

After about 45 minutes, Gregg got out his tools. We decided to permanently break the oven door by bending it with a crowbar-like thing that gave us about a 12-inch opening. Just enough space for Gregg to spear the turkey with two roasting forks and squeeze the bird through the opening and onto the platter.

Thankfully, the turkey was fully cooked and tasted wonderful. Crisis averted…at the expense of my oven.

Your Thanksgiving turkey most likely hasn't been trapped in your oven. But chances are you've felt trapped before. Held captive by something – negative thoughts, bad attitudes, destructive habits, harmful patterns. As desperate as you desire to be free, you just can't seem to find a way out. And the harder you try, the more entangled you become.

In the letter Paul wrote to the Galatians, he reminds them of their freedom in Christ. *"It is for freedom that Christ has set us free. Stand firm, then, and do not let yourselves be burdened again by a yoke of slavery."* Galatians 5:1

It's not freedom they earned or deserve; it's solely God's grace working through our faith in the work of Christ that we receive this freedom.

Jesus has set us free. Through His blood, He has provided an escape for us. It's not something we can arrive at on our willpower by trying harder or doing better. It's a gift. Through the work of Christ, we receive it. And like any gift we receive, we should do so gratefully.

This freedom isn't a license to live however we please or do whatever we desire. It's a freedom Christ purchased with His very own blood. We can now live in the freedom in which God created us to live. It's freedom from sin, freedom from having to earn our way to God, and freedom from guilt and condemnation.

Best yet, it's a freedom that will eventually provide a way for us to spend eternity in the presence of the Father.

Stand firm. Stand strong. By God's grace, you are free. As you dwell on this truth, I pray you will remember these words from Paul and take time to thank God for providing a way to freedom for you.

Day Two – Cages

Shortly after we were married, Gregg and I saw the most unusual and unlikely sight while running errands in downtown Honolulu. It was one of those "rub your eyes to make sure you're not seeing things" kind of things. We looked at each other to confirm what we'd just witnessed.

We couldn't believe our eyes. While sitting at a stoplight, an elephant ran past us.

Yes, you heard me correctly.

An elephant!

In Hawaii.

Running loose down the street.

(For your information, we have a lot of exotic animals here, but no wild elephants. And certainly, no animals of that magnitude roaming freely through downtown.)

Tyke, the circus elephant, had grown tired of spending years living in captivity and made a break for freedom.

Sometimes to step towards freedom, we must get sick of life in captivity.

To have the courage to change, we must become fed up with living in our "cages". As much as God desires for us to live in freedom, and as much as we say we want freedom, there is something comforting about our "cage". We've been there so long we can't imagine life differently.

Bound by insecurity.

Stuck in shame.

Held captive by negative thoughts.

Ensnared by unbridled emotions.

God created you to live in freedom and wholeness, but He presents you with a choice as to how you will live in relationship with Him. You can choose to trust God and live under His loving leadership, or you can be the master of your own life.

It's a brave step you must take. In the cage, you are your master. Stepping out of the cage, you relinquish control but gain so much more. Let me explain…

God created us in His image and likeness. He designated us as representatives of God's rule on earth. But early on, scripture tells us things went wrong…terribly, irreparably wrong.

Genesis 1 describes the origin of a perfect world where God's first created humans, Adam and Eve, enjoyed such an intimate relationship with God and each other that they were *naked and unashamed* (Genesis 1:26-31, 2:25)

In Genesis 3, things begin to unravel, *"Now the serpent was more crafty than any of the wild animals the* LORD *God had made. He said to the woman, 'Did God really say, "You must not eat from any tree in the garden"?'"* Genesis 3:1

Seeds of doubt, kernels of deception planted in our hearts, breed bondage. When you believe a lie about yourself, a lie about God, you take a step away from freedom into a trap perfectly set for you by the enemy.

What begins as a faint whisper slowly begins to shape your soul. Perhaps you've heard the murmuring…

- God isn't a good God.
- He doesn't love me.
- Nobody cares about me.
- I'm not worth anything.
- I'll never be enough.
- I don't have what it takes.
- I can't help the way I am.
- My sin isn't that bad.

250

The enemy's plan is to convince us to believe lies rather than the truth. These lies begin to influence what we think, how we feel, and how we behave.

In Genesis 3, the deception fed to Eve was *you will be free if you break free from God.*

How often do I believe the same lie – trying to find freedom apart from God? Thinking that other things, achievements, and relationships will satisfy us and lead us to a rich and satisfying life.

Why do I think I know better?

Why do I attempt to pursue freedom apart from the wisdom of a loving God?

When we reject God and choose to be the master of our own life, we're left vulnerable, entangled, and exposed instead of experiencing the freedom and protection we're looking for.

"Then the eyes of both of them were opened, and they realized they were naked; so they sewed fig leaves together and made coverings for themselves." Genesis 3:7

Because we live in a fallen world and nobody's perfect, we've all experienced the vulnerability and shame that comes from sin. We've developed habits and patterns to cope with life. We've all created our "fig leaves" to cover up, and we've become really good at hiding and hunkering down in our "cages".

Thankfully, God is the master *hide-and-seek* player. There's nowhere we can go to escape His loving reach.

When you turn to Christ and receive God's loving rule and lordship, you enter an intimate relationship where you're known and loved by God just as you are – broken and vulnerable – and you feel no shame.

Jesus is the one who covers your shame. He opens the door of your "cage" and lovingly leads you to freedom.

Freedom comes when we're not hiding. Freedom comes when we're truthful about our needs. Freedom comes when we realize God sees our sin, brokenness, and imperfections and loves us anyway.

Paul explains it this way, *"Blessed are those whose transgressions are forgiven, whose sins are covered."* Romans 4:7

Instead of cowering in your cage, let Jesus cover you. That's the path out of captivity into true freedom.

Day Three – Travel Light

Confession time…I'm not a light traveler. I always overpack. My motto for travel is, "If you think you may need it, bring it."

I'm pretty sure you'd be embarrassed by all the gear we cart around on our family vacations – surfboards, wetsuits, skateboards, bodyboards, fins, and the extra bag to bring home an abundance of Trader Joe's snacks. Of course, this is in addition to the clothes, toiletries, books, and whatever it takes to keep our family running for two weeks. (If you ever find yourself behind us in the TSA line, you've been warned.) But when I go for my daily run, I travel differently. I leave everything at home so I can have the energy and endurance to run unencumbered.

Competitive runners will even determine their clothes by choosing outfits that give them the least resistance as they compete. If anything threatens to hinder the effectiveness of their performance, they get rid of it.

God has a race for you to run. It's why He created you, and He doesn't want you trying to run your race while attempting to carry a big suitcase chock full of baggage. He wants you to run free and unhindered.

However, we tend to collect baggage and carry it with us as we run through life. We pick up attitudes, habits, and behaviors and seem to have difficulty letting go of them. To run fast and free, we must be willing to let go of some things.

The writer of Hebrews explained it this way, *"Therefore, since we are surrounded by such a huge crowd of witnesses to the life of faith, let us strip off every weight that slows us down, especially the sin that so easily trips us up. And let us run with endurance the race God has set before us. We do this by keeping our eyes on Jesus, the champion who initiates and perfects our faith."* Hebrews 12:1-2a NLT

This passage refers to the many people who have gone before us and modeled what it looks like to live free and full of faith. Their lives serve as an example and encouragement as we persevere in our race. Our response to their example is to run the best race we can run. This requires us to eliminate the things hindering our ability to do that.

Sometimes it's a sin in our lives that we need to get rid of. As much as I like to believe I can resist the temptation to sin, I'm aware of how it can easily trip me up and enslave me before I even realize it. If I don't want to eat an entire bag of Oreos, I probably shouldn't buy them in the first place.

Sometimes the things slowing us down aren't necessarily bad, but they weigh us down and keep us from living at our best. They turn our attention and affection away from Christ, gradually becoming more important than God.

While the writer doesn't detail what these "weights" are, two of the things that weigh me down the most are distractions and busyness. Our world is filled with distractions. It's hard to *fix our eyes* on Christ when our attention shifts to every shiny object that enters our periphery.

In his book, *The Ruthless Elimination of Hurry,* John Mark Comer writes, "What you give your attention to is the person you become."[1]

You can't run fast if you're weighed down and distracted. That's why the enemy works so hard to keep us in bondage. He knows the power our lives will have when we're free and focused on Christ.

Holocaust survivor Corrie Ten Boom acknowledged that "if the devil can't make you bad, he'll make you busy."[2] The enemy knows that a busy and distracted life severs connection with God and makes us less attentive to the needs around us.

God longs to bring life, freedom, truth, and purpose to your life, but the devil works hard to destroy anything good, anything of God. Whether it's the slavery sin brings or the weights of distraction and busyness slowing us down, we're empowered to run free when we throw them aside and fix our focus firmly on Jesus.

Day Four – Baby Steps

Think with me for a moment about all the routine tasks you do every day: brushing your teeth, driving your car, getting dressed, putting on makeup, taking notes in class, making dinner, changing a diaper...Got some in mind?

Now imagine what it would be like to do those simple tasks while restrained by handcuffs. It would be difficult—if not *impossible*—to complete some of the little things we take for granted and do every day. Yet often, as Christians, we attempt to do something very similar.

We desire to live our lives for God. With good intentions, we attempt to fulfill what He has created us to do but find ourselves stumbling around because we're still hindered by habits, bound by bad attitudes, and burdened by the effects of sin.

Perhaps you may feel so hopeless that you can't even see where the path to freedom begins. After living a certain way for a long time, we can get so used to the oppression that we can't imagine being any different.

Recognizing and acknowledging the things hindering us are the first steps toward freedom. Living in denial, remaining unaware – will only continue to keep us trapped and bound.

Where do we begin to break the chains and chart a new course toward freedom? Here are some baby steps to get you on a journey toward freedom.

Truth – Fill your life with truth. One of the lies the enemy wants us to believe is that we will always be a certain way because we are that way now.

It doesn't matter if you have been bound by fear or plagued with insecurity or whether you have an eating disorder or a family history of alcoholism. God can change you; He can set you free!

Throughout the Bible, we see that when people encountered God, their lives were transformed. As you draw close to Jesus and fix your eyes on Him, His truth penetrates your heart.

While the devil cannot stop you from living in the freedom Christ offers, he is masterful at accusing, condemning, and deceiving us. It's been said that we have an estimated 30,000 thoughts a day, and 70% of them are negative ones.[3]

The enemy will bombard our minds with negative thoughts all day long. We often receive these thoughts as the truth and allow them to shape our lives. It's essential for us to allow the truth of God's Word to define us instead of the devil's lies and accusations.

Thoughts like, *"I've tried before, but it's never worked,"* or *"My mom and dad were like this, so I'll always be this way",* or *"Maybe other people can change, but not me,"* are lies designed to convince you to doubt God's power and promises and keep you lugging around the same baggage year after year.

I realize some battles require the help of trusted counselors and sometimes medication. If you're struggling with depression, anxiety, trauma, addiction, or something similar, you don't have to fight alone. Talk to someone. Seek professional help.

The battle for your freedom is fierce. Whatever you're facing, the best weapon you possess to fight with is God's Word. Reading the Bible every day is essential to living free. When we meditate on God's Word, we encounter truth – the truth about God and who He's created us to be.

Slowly, the grip sin and darkness have in our lives begins to loosen. God's Word – active and alive in us – recalibrates our hearts and empowers us to reject the lies.

But it's not enough to merely *know* the truth and expect change to magically happen. We must do our part.

Turn – Turn from sin. Seeing the truth will lead you to a place of repentance. You'll desire to change and have the motivation to live differently.

Sometimes, we cannot maintain freedom over sin because the past is still an option for us. We cannot keep our past sin as a "plan B" and expect to live in freedom.

When you choose to willfully disobey God, you give the enemy access to your life. The enemy has no authority in our life. The only power he has is the power we give to him through our sin and disobedience.

God has the power to transform your life, but it begins when you reject the lies, stop making excuses, and embrace the truth. Jesus said it this way to those who were following Him, *"To the Jews who had believed him, Jesus said, 'If you hold to my teaching, you are really my disciples.* [32] *Then you will know the truth, and the truth will set you free.'"* John 8:31-32

You no longer have to live under the burden of the law or in bondage to sin. When the truth of the Gospel penetrates your heart, and you begin to see yourself as completely sinful and broken, standing before a merciful and gracious God, the natural responses are gratitude and repentance.

Reject the lies of guilt and condemnation and replace them with God's truth. Turn from sin and begin to walk in a new direction. Every day, take a step.

Trust – Jesus sets you free. Trust in what Jesus accomplished when he died on the cross for you and receive His power to walk in a new direction. If you take one small step in a new direction every day, think how far you'll travel in a year…five years…ten years…over your lifetime?

When you place your trust in God, you are putting into practice what Jesus taught. You're living a life of faith. Trusting in Christ has a practical outworking on our attitude, actions, thoughts, and behavior.

Truth…turn…trust. Baby steps in a new direction begin the life-long process of being transformed by the Holy Spirit and being shaped into the image of Christ.

You are free, and your future will be determined not by your past, not by your present, but by your passionate pursuit of God. Break off those shackles and embrace the freedom made available to you in Christ one step, one day at a time.

Day Five – Living Free

When Harriet Tubman was born, the law stated that every child born to an enslaved woman would be enslaved as well. Because her mother was enslaved, she was enslaved. She inherited this atrocity at birth.

Harriet dreamt of a life of freedom. But freedom wouldn't be given to her; it was something she had to pursue courageously.

Harriet concluded that the risk of pursuing freedom outweighed her desire to remain in bondage. Moved by the hope of a new and better future, she forged nearly 90 miles, by herself, until finally stepping across the border into Pennsylvania and experiencing true freedom for the very first time.[4]

Harriet's determination led her to pursue freedom for herself. It also motivated her to lead dozens more to freedom through her courageous leadership on the Underground Railroad.

Sometimes it's through the pain of living in slavery that we gather the courage to move toward freedom. Sometimes it's seeing others make the journey that we gain the determination to step out ourselves.

Thankfully, God doesn't ask for us to stage our jailbreak. He holds the keys that can release us from our bondage. He longs to bring freedom to areas in your life that have been subjected to years of darkness and captivity.

It's something He loves to do! The prophet Isaiah speaks with anticipation about the ministry of the coming Messiah.

"The Spirit of the Sovereign LORD is on me, because the LORD has anointed me to proclaim good news to the poor. He has sent me to bind up the brokenhearted, to proclaim freedom for the captives and release from darkness for the prisoners, ² to proclaim the year of the LORD's favor and the day of vengeance of

our God, to comfort all who mourn, ³ and provide for those who grieve in Zion—to bestow on them a crown of beauty instead of ashes, the oil of joy instead of mourning, and a garment of praise instead of a spirit of despair. They will be called oaks of righteousness, a planting of the LORD for the display of his splendor. ⁴ They will rebuild the ancient ruins and restore the places long devastated; they will renew the ruined cities that have been devastated for generations." Isaiah 61:1-4

Perhaps, you need a little "good news". Or possibly you could use some comforting. Maybe you're desperate for freedom from dark areas in your life.

Whatever your need, wherever your hurt, whatever your bondage, a large part of Jesus' ministry was to heal, comfort, and set free those held captive by the enemy (see also Luke 4:18).

Let's look at verse three a little more closely to see what Jesus provides for you.

- A crown of beauty *instead of* ashes...
- Oil of joy *instead of* mourning...
- A garment of praise *instead of* a spirit of despair.

Your life right now may resemble ashes, mourning, and despair more closely than beauty, joy, and praise. The good news is that God can restore any heartache or trauma that has left you barren and bankrupt and infuse it with His abundant life, freedom, and healing.

The horrific exploitation and violation of women and children is an all too present reality in our culture. Even more disturbing is when these events are covered up, excused, or swept under the rug (see 2 Samuel 13:1-20). The emotional trauma that remains can be just as haunting as the physical violation.

Perhaps, you've experienced this. If so, I am deeply sorry. God, in His rich mercy, can remove your shame. He can heal the wounded places of your soul and make you whole again. He can take your despair, pain, and shame and make you feel beautiful and pure. He can restore the virtue and dignity you are worthy of as His daughter.

I know I mentioned it yesterday, but it bears repeating. Often, pursuing healing in this area necessitates professional help. Please talk with someone. God uses other people to bring health, wholeness, and restoration. Don't be too embarrassed to avoid getting the support you need to go forward.

My in-laws live in Lake Tahoe, a place filled with majestic trees. I enjoy running the trails behind their house to admire their strength and beauty. These Tahoe pines endure a cold, harsh winter every year yet continue to stand firm, never ceasing to display God's splendor.

I love how this scripture passage in Isaiah paints a picture of a life restored: *"They will be called oaks of righteousness, a planting of the LORD for the display of his splendor."* (Verse 3)

God desires to build something solid and healthy in your life. He can use your desolate winter seasons to create something beautiful. All your suffering, pain, and bondage, when fully yielded to the Lord, is an opportunity for God's power, grace, and glory to be revealed through your life.

The transformation doesn't stop there. God's grace and power can resurrect areas in your life that have been desolate for generations. *"They will rebuild the ancient ruins and restore the places long devastated; they will renew the ruined cities that have been devastated for generations."* (Verse 4)

In the area surrounding Lake Tahoe, there are several ghost towns. These old towns scattered throughout the West used to bustle with activity and promise during the gold and silver rushes in the 1800s. Now, except for the tourists who visit them, they are desolate and empty.

Towns that once held so much life and promise sit hopelessly dead and barren. Much effort has been made to preserve them, but they will never be restored to the position of grandeur and prestige they once held.

Unfortunately, because of sin, there may be areas of barren wasteland in our life. Sometimes these areas remain undisturbed or haven't been dealt with for generations! Like the ghost towns, they are dry, desolate, and unfruitful. You may be so used to them that you're unaware of their effect on you.

God can restore the barren and unfruitful areas of our lives. Jesus can rebuild the ruins that have destroyed your family for generations. You don't have to live with bondage; your children don't have to live with that bondage.

Eric Liddell, Olympic athlete and missionary to China, said, *"Circumstances may appear to wreck our lives and God's plans. But God is not helpless among the ruins. God's love is still working. He comes in, He takes the calamity, uses it victoriously, working out His wonderful plan of love."* [5]

My sister, God is not helpless among the ruins. He is at work, restoring and crafting His wonderful plan for your life. You can move forward. You can live free.

14

You are Victorious

Day One – No Longer Slaves

For four hundred years, the Israelites lived as slaves in Egypt. The more desperately they cried out to God, the more unbearable their burdens became.

The Egyptians hated them and worked them ruthlessly, making their lives miserable. They had lost their freedom, and now Pharaoh wanted their families as well, ordering all the Israelite babies to be drowned in the Nile River.

When would God answer their cry for help? Day after day, year after year, they dreamed of someday being free.

During this bitter season of suffering, God raised up a deliverer in their midst. God had told Moses He had special land for the Israelites. A land they could call their *own*. It was an abundant land, described as flowing with milk and honey. Moses was the man God chose to lead them to their new home.

Finally, hope was alive for Israel! God loosened Pharoah's grip by performing miracles, sending the Egyptian people ten plagues of hardship, disaster, and sickness.

Despite the devastation throughout Egypt, Pharaoh remained committed to holding the Israelites in bondage, refusing to let them leave. Until one night, God sent a final plague, a finishing blow, which killed every firstborn Egyptian son. God broke the strength of Pharaoh's will, and the Israelites were finally free to go.

What a range of emotions they must have experienced. The delight and joy of finally being free; the awe and wonder upon seeing and experiencing God's power; the uncertainty regarding what lies ahead; and perhaps even a little sadness in having to leave the only home they had ever known.

It didn't take long for them to realize that their new freedom didn't mean a life of ease and comfort. But God went with them every step of the way. He showed His presence among them by providing a cloud during the day and a pillar of fire by night.

With all God had done for them, with His visible presence and active involvement among them, you would think they would have wholeheartedly and unquestionably followed Him. Not so.

They were hot, hungry, thirsty (never a good combination for cheerful dispositions and teamwork), and traveling as an army of over six hundred thousand men, not including the women and children (see Exodus 12:37). (And suddenly my travel challenges appear so small.)

They grumbled. They complained about everything. They argued. They refused to embrace what God had for them.

They quickly forgot everything the Lord had done for them and settled for a life of wandering in the wilderness. They even began expressing a desire to return to Egypt (Numbers 14:1-4)!

But they didn't give up. They persevered and pressed in to receive God's promise. After forty years of wandering in the wilderness, God speaks to Moses.

"When we were at Mount Sinai, the LORD our God said to us, 'You have stayed at this mountain long enough. ⁷ It is time to break camp and move on... ⁸ Look, I am giving all this land to you! Go in and occupy it, for it is the land the LORD swore to give to your ancestors Abraham, Isaac, and Jacob, and to all their descendants.'" Deuteronomy 1:6-8 NLT

Years ago, while reading this passage, these words jumped out and grabbed me. It was a difficult season for our family, and I struggled to see how God could work through our situation.

Looking back, I see how I had become comfortable, had settled into a routine, and had shrunk my expectations of what God could do in my life.

I hadn't stopped reading my Bible or attending church. I wasn't entangled in a secret life of sin. It was something more subtle but still very dangerous. My passion had dwindled. I had stopped fighting for more of God's presence in my life. I had become comfortable camping on the mountain while God desired much more.

It was a defining moment for me. I realized that I didn't want to stay in the wilderness. I didn't want a comfortable life. I wanted to become everything God created me to be.

How about you? Are you camping on the mountain when God has a Promised Land for you to enter? Are there areas in your life you've grown complacent?

That day, God changed me. He changed my perspective and birthed in my heart a determination to aggressively fight for everything God has for my family and me. He can do the same for you. You don't have to live in defeat any longer. You can live victoriously, but it won't come without a fight.

Day Two – Shark Fighting

Not too long ago, one of my kids came into my room and announced, *"Hey, mom, I'm going to the North Shore to swim with sharks. I'll see you later."*

Huh?

Supposedly, there's a guy on the North Shore who people PAY to take them on a snorkeling experience where they are swimming with sharks.

I probed my teen a little further...

"You mean the smaller dwarf sharks, right?"

"No, mom (cue exasperated sigh and eye roll), *these are real sharks about six feet long."*

As my heartbeat quickened, I pressed, *"So, you'll be in one of those protective cage thingys, right?"*

Repeat the exasperated sigh and eye roll, *"Moooommmmm, most sharks aren't aggressive and don't bother you if you don't bother them."*

My son assured me that he and his friends would be diving in an area where the sharks are friendly, don't bother people, and don't mind you swimming up in their business.

Who would want to do such a thing?

Apparently, my kids. Yes, I said *kids*, as in the plural form. More than one of my little offspring has willingly jumped into shark-infested waters and paid significant money to do it.

Lord, teach me how to pray.

Australian professional surfer, Mick Fanning, knows what it's like to come face to face with a shark and live to talk about it.

As a three-time world title winner, he's spent a large portion of his life in the ocean. In 2015, in the final heat after a long day of competing at Jeffreys Bay off the coast of South Africa, hundreds of fans watching from the shore saw something they're likely never to forget.

Out of nowhere, a shark emerged, knocking Fanning off his surfboard and quickly pulling him underwater. But Fanning wasn't about to succumb to the shark; he got back on his board, punched the shark, and swam to the safety of the rescue crew.

A National Geographic article described it this way, *Fanning also appeared to stay calm and "did everything right" during the brief attack. It looked like he put the board between him and the shark, he avoided the mouth, he struck the shark, and then moved away. Sharks are known to respect size and power in the water, and experts say the best thing to do if you are approached by one is punch it hard. Aim for the nose, the eyes, or the gills, which are particularly sensitive, if possible.*[1]

Good to know.

Most likely, you won't find yourself in shark-infested waters fighting for your life. However, you'll have some "sharks" circling you at some point. When fear, anxiety, hopelessness, darkness, and defeat rear their ugly heads and attempt to devour you, take your cues from Mick Fanning.

Fight the shark. There is a well-known saying that says, *whatever is worth having, is worth fighting for.*

In her book *Believing God*, Beth Moore writes that victory assumes a counterpart defeat. You can't have victory without an opponent and you can't be more than conquerors with nothing to conquer.[2]

You have a tough opponent who wants to keep you trapped in a never-ending cycle of defeat, fear, and hopelessness. But God, in His grace and mercy, promises to help.

When you feel like the sharks are circling and dragging you under, don't give up! Don't yield or surrender. Fight. Punch it hard…with everything you got. Muster up your courage and know you're not alone in the fight. God is right there fighting with you.

Sometimes we get so fixated on the "sharks" swimming around us that we forget our power and authority as Christ-followers. The apostle Paul reminds the Ephesian church,

"A final word: Be strong in the Lord and in his mighty power. [11] Put on all of God's armor so that you will be able to stand firm against all strategies of the devil. [12] For we are not fighting against flesh-and-blood enemies, but against evil rulers and authorities of the unseen world, against mighty powers in this dark world, and against evil spirits in the heavenly places. [13] Therefore, put on every piece of God's armor so you will be able to resist the enemy in the time of evil. Then after the battle you will still be standing firm." Ephesians 6:10-13 NLT

God's power is so much greater than our human effort. Our ability to fight and be victorious has nothing to do with our strength and everything to do with the strength God displays through us. God supplies us with an armor of protection and offensive weapons of the Word and prayer to fight.

Secondly, don't surf alone.

Within seconds of being tossed around by a shark, Fanning was rescued and pulled to safety by the nearby lifeguards on jet skis. How foolish would it have been if he denied their help, saying, *"No thanks, I've got this."* What would've happened if he was all alone in the water!?

When we find ourselves beaten down and battered by the sharks in our lives, we often think we have to tough it out on our own. We hesitate to ask for help because we don't want to be a burden or appear weak.

Community is that beautiful place where we don't have to have it all together all the time. When we're weak, others are there to strengthen us. And when we're riding the waves and swimming strong, we can rescue others who are being devoured by the sharks circling their lives.

Ecclesiastes describes it this way, *"Two people are better off than one, for they can help each other succeed. ¹⁰ If one person falls, the other can reach out and help. But someone who falls alone is in real trouble."* Ecclesiastes 4:9-10 NLT

You don't have to fight alone. Call a lifeline, phone a friend, and get help. Surround yourself with people who will fight for you and fight with you.

So, the next time the sharks start circling, and you feel as if you're defeated, devoured, and like you're drowning, remember this last shark fighting tip: *don't be passive.* You have all you need to fight back and emerge from the water victorious.

Day Three – Baby Sharks

Let's return to our story of the Israelites and their wanderings through the wilderness. It used to baffle me why an eleven-day journey took forty years. God delivered them from Egypt with such a display of miraculous power. They should have been able to cross the Jordan River and get on with their lives! But God, in His wisdom, knew that a quick trip to the Promised Land would lead to more problems later. So, He took them on the scenic route.

God knew the Israelites would return to Egypt if they encountered enemies and had to fight. While slavery was miserable, it was safe if they did their job. For over four hundred years, they hadn't faced war or fought a battle (Exodus 13:17-18). They weren't prepared for what God had planned for them.

Their hearts and minds had to change to be successful and prosperous in the land God was giving them. During their wilderness wanderings, God was building strength in them and getting them ready for battle.

Some of the "sharks" circling our lives are obvious ones, like fear, worry, and anxiety, while others are more subtle, like *baby sharks* (doo doo doo doo doo). Sorry, I couldn't resist. Young moms, you'll have that song swirling in your heads for the rest of the day. You're welcome.

Don't be fooled. Even though these baby sharks appear harmless, they are just as dangerous. Let's look at a few of these "baby sharks", as I believe these can also drag us down.

Impatience (Numbers 21:4-6)

Following God's mighty display of power and deliverance from Egypt, you think the Israelites would have been convinced of God's ability and desire to care for them. But the people grew impatient with how long the journey was taking.

They had a timetable, and God wasn't doing things at the speed or manner they thought He should. *"They traveled from Mount Hor along the route to the Red Sea, to go around Edom. But the people grew impatient on the way; ⁵ they spoke against God and against Moses, and said, "Why have you brought us up out of Egypt to die in the wilderness?"* Numbers 21:4-5

The Jewish people did what I sometimes find myself doing when God doesn't do things when and how I think they should be done. They threw a tantrum at the level of a three-year-old toddler in the middle of Target. They were okay with God's plan of *deliverance from slavery and inheritance of the Promised Land* until they had to wait for it and work for it.

Ouch, waiting and working…two incredibly hard things for my soul, which seeks the immediate and easy. The people's impatience led them to speak against God, despising His provision and rejecting His servant, Moses.

Think about it. When we become impatient, aren't we following in their footsteps? We may not *say it*, but we're subtly communicating that God should be serving us and meeting our needs.

God's response? He sent snakes, people! Ugly, slithery, creepy, venomous snakes. Remember this next time you find yourself waiting in the extra-long line at the grocery store.

Which leads to another "baby shark" we often encounter…

Complaining (Exodus 16:2)

(I realize we've already talked about this twice, but ladies, let's just admit, this is a biggy for us.)

As a mom, I deal with unsatisfied customers every day. Whether it's what I choose to serve for dinner or whose turn it is to pick up the dogs' doo-doo, there's occasionally someone in our family who is unhappy with my decision and makes their opinion known. (And yes, I admit that sometimes I am the one who feels compelled to voice my dissatisfaction.)

The Israelites' attitude downright stunk during much of their time in the wilderness. From the time Pharaoh let them go, nothing seemed to please them, satisfy them, or meet their approval. A critical, complaining attitude contributed to the length of time they spent in the wilderness. While they were looking to their circumstances to satisfy them, God was the One who wanted to satisfy them. "*In the desert the whole community grumbled against Moses and Aaron.*" Exodus 16:2

Remember back in Chapter One, we discovered that when we complain, we're expressing dissatisfaction that God's provision isn't enough.

A complaining attitude hinders God's ability to use us while simultaneously making us miserable. A double whammy! Nothing pleases us, and nothing meets our selfish satisfaction. Not the kind of people you want to be around.

These are just a couple of lessons we can learn from the Israelites, who discovered the hard way that impatience and complaining will rob you of the *right now*. God has rich purpose and value in every season. When we fritter it away by comparing ourselves to everyone else and expressing dissatisfaction with our circumstances, our souls become restless and dissatisfied with God's provision.

While it's important to dream about the future and learn from past mistakes, we can't let these things distract us from the present. Fight back those "baby sharks" so you can step into the richness of what God has for you right now.

Day Four – Don't Give Up

I had unpacked our last box just weeks before when Gregg came home from the office looking a little defeated.

I asked him how his day of meetings went, and he responded by quoting a scripture David prayed in Psalm 27, *"I would have despaired unless I had believed that I would see the goodness of the LORD in the land of the living."* Psalm 27:13

We were in the middle of a stressful and challenging ministry situation; our future was uncertain, and we didn't have a clear path forward. Living with relational tension, financial strain, and emotional stress was taking a toll on us, and we were discouraged. Oh, and did I mention that I was also pregnant?

As followers of Christ, we're not immune to discouragement. Throughout Scripture, we learn how God's people responded in the face of crisis – some leaned into the challenge, while others, at times, shrunk back.

Please don't misunderstand me… Sometimes even the most faith-filled, positive person becomes discouraged. Experiencing discouragement isn't a commentary on your relationship with God; it doesn't mean you just need more faith. The difference maker is how you will choose to respond.

Discouragement has been described as a loss of confidence and an absence of enthusiasm. It's when your zest for life takes an emotional hit, and you struggle to see your life through a lens of hope and optimism.

A scary thing about discouragement is how contagious it can be. We look at our circumstances and predetermine that what we're facing is impossible to overcome. Discouraging thoughts like, *"I can't do it"*, *"This is impossible"*, *"I'll never be able to"*, or *"Things will never change"*, are all lies from the enemy to try to get you to give up before you even begin!

In Numbers 13, discouragement prompted all the spies, except Joshua and Caleb, to give up. The attitude of the spies influenced and affected the whole camp. They thought what God was asking of them was impossible. The people were giants, and they seemed so small! How could they defeat them?

But if God has called you to do something, He will help you accomplish the task. It may not be easy, but His grace and strength will be sufficient.

In 1 Kings 18-19, the prophet Elijah had just experienced one of his greatest victories when God worked through him to display God's power over the prophets of Baal. You would think that if ANYONE was immune to discouragement, it would be a prophet who God had just used to reveal God's power to an entire nation.

However, upon arriving home, Elijah experienced such fear and discouragement that he fled, traveling over one hundred miles to hide, praying to God that he would die. Within twenty-four hours, he went from being used by God to demonstrate one of the biggest miracles recorded in the Bible to completely losing confidence in God, concluding his work was ineffective, and his life wasn't worth living.

Pretty dark, right?

Sometimes the battle seems so great that we can't imagine how God will get us through the storm. Perhaps you've been living with a degree of darkness and discouragement for a while now.

If so, you're not alone. The prolonged Covid pandemic has weakened our resistance and diminished our ability to fight. Collectively, as a world, we've experienced varying degrees of trauma. How do we move forward?

Let me clarify that being discouraged and living with depression are different emotions that require different responses. I can't prescribe you a quick antidote for depression. If you're struggling with depression, call a trusted friend, small group leader, or a counselor in your community. Don't put it off, and don't try to navigate it alone.

But as for the seasons of discouragement that we all experience? How do we move forward? How do we stir our faith and raise our hope again?

The tendency in those seasons is to ask God to get us out of our current situation – we wallow, we retreat, and we run (like Elijah) – instead of inviting God into the storm.

Think about it, throughout Scripture, most of the time, God didn't rescue His people from their crisis. Instead, He came to be with them and walk with them through it. Israel in the wilderness (Exodus 13:21), Daniel's friends in the fiery furnace (Daniel 3), Jeremiah in exile (Jeremiah 43), and the disciples in the storm (Mark 4:35-41) were not examples of miraculous rescues, but illustrations of God's sustaining grace when we need it the most.

God said it this way through the prophet Isaiah, *"Don't be afraid, for I am with you. Don't be discouraged, for I am your God. I will strengthen you and help you. I will hold you up with my victorious right hand."* Isaiah 41:10

My friend, when the dark cloud of discouragement begins to envelop you, don't retreat or run away. Invite God into the moment. You can have courage knowing that as you walk through the darkness, you don't walk alone.

Day Five – A Gold Medal

One of our beloved family activities is game night and we have a few favorite board games we pull out from time to time. Most of the time, there's lots of laughter and quality time connecting.

But I'll be honest. There have been occasions when the competitive personalities of seven people take over, and our festive, family-bonding game night devolves into an evening of arguing, accusations, and alleged tactics of foul play.

No one likes to lose. Perhaps that's why stories about an underdog pulling off an unimaginable upset inspire us profoundly and emotionally.

In the 1972 Olympics, Finnish policeman, Lasse Viren, stumbled and fell just before the halfway point in the 10,000m final. While most would consider their hopes of winning gold to be gone at that point, instead of giving up, Viren quickly rose to his feet and calmly, persistently kept running.

Determined not to give up, he kept going. Little by little, meter by meter, Viren made up for the lost time. Not only did he decisively win the gold medal, but he also set a world record! [3]

What if we lived with a similar kind of calm determination? One that has resilience when life gets tough. One that persists through challenges and presses into God.

Dear friend, God has a race for you to run. Will it be challenging at times? Absolutely. Will you trip and fall sometimes? Yes. Will there be seasons when you want to quit? Most likely.

In his letter to the Corinthians, Paul knew the pressure and toll difficult seasons could have on people. The early Christians were persecuted, pressured, and pushed to their limit. Yet, he encourages them to keep running, to keep fighting. *"Therefore, since God in his mercy has given us this new way, we never give up."* 2 Corinthians 4:1 NLT

I love that. Paul encourages them to make up their mind on the front end never to give up. You may not win a gold medal, but you'll gain something even more precious.

As Paul closes this chapter, he tells them why they need to keep going. He reminds them what they're fighting for. *"For our light and momentary troubles are achieving for us an eternal glory that far outweighs them all. [18] So we fix our eyes not on what is seen, but on what is unseen, since what is seen is temporary, but what is unseen is eternal."* 2 Corinthians 4:17-18

When darkness descends on our lives, our visibility is restricted. We can't see into the future because our gaze is fixated on the challenges right in front of us.

Paul is encouraging the believers to think of every hardship and every challenge as an opportunity to glorify God and prepare them to receive their eternal inheritance.

To do this, Paul instructs them to shift their focus. Our focus matters. Where is your focus right now?

- A difficult work situation?
- Financial problems?
- Relational conflicts?
- Issues with your kids?
- Marital struggle?
- Health complications?

Don't get me wrong. I'm not saying we neglect these things. They are valid areas of concern. But in every challenge, there is also an opportunity. We can resist and struggle until we get through it, or we can invite God into our crisis and choose to grow through it. To do this, we must shift our perspective. That's what Paul is trying to teach the Corinthian people to do.

When we shift our focus from being fixated on our troubles to Christ, His power, and the future glory we'll experience with Him in eternity, our troubles may not completely go away, but our ability to navigate through them with faith and hope increases.

We feel His presence. We tap into His power. We have an assurance that He is with us. We're not alone. The Holy Spirit is at work through our lives.

In another letter, Paul reminds the Christians in Rome, *"Who shall separate us from the love of Christ? Shall trouble or hardship or persecution or famine or nakedness or danger or sword? 36 As it is written: 'For your sake we face death all day long; we are considered as sheep to be slaughtered.' 37 No, in all these things we are more than conquerors through him who loved us."* Romans 8:35-38

Nothing separates us from God's immense love! We are more than conquerors, and He has promised to walk with you through the dark seasons of life to a place of victory. The final episode has been filmed, and God wins—big.

This doesn't mean everything will turn out as you planned or desired. It doesn't mean that you'll never suffer or experience conflict; it doesn't mean you'll always be financially secure or have a clean bill of health.

But as you fix your eyes on the unseen glory of Christ waiting for you in eternity, you'll experience His presence with you, leading and guiding you every step of the way. You'll feel His strength and grace sustaining you, and before you know it, you'll be through it and have stronger faith. You'll have experienced the faithfulness of God, and it will build your resilience and hope when you encounter another valley you must walk through.

Don't give up. Keep moving forward – even if it's one step at a time. God is with you, and He will sustain you. You will get through this. And one day, when you enter God's glory, you will stand before Him, and He will present you with an even greater *gold medal.* An eternal glory that far outweighs anything you could experience or obtain this side of heaven.

15

You are Fulfilled

Day One – Construction Zone

I think you'll appreciate the unusual epitaph marking Ruth Bell Graham's grave marker. It reads, *"End of construction. Thank you for your patience."* She saw this phrase on a highway construction sign and commented that it reminded her of God's patient care in preparing her for heaven.[1]

Sometimes it seems like God's work in our life brings continual construction work, doesn't it? It's noisy, inconvenient, messy, and uncomfortable. Yet, it's an invaluable part of God's process of shaping us to be more like Jesus.

While I would prefer God's work in me to be accomplished

comfortably and painlessly, most of the time, God's shaping and molding in my life have required something stronger, more like a jackhammer. Although it's a process that won't be completed this side of heaven, until then, we can learn to enjoy, grow through, and be grateful for the journey.

As we work towards the completion of this study, I pray that God brought some helpful *construction* into your life. He's most certainly done that in mine. I'm so thankful for the work He's begun, and I trust God will continue His work in your life for years to come.

God doesn't want us to navigate our lives around a bunch of potholes. He desires to fill every area of your life – every puka (that's what we call "hole" here in Hawaii), every crack, every fissure.

Yet, wholeness and fulfillment can seem elusive at times. As we work through our last chapter together, let's explore what it means to be truly fulfilled in life and how we can start to experience it at a profoundly deep level.

Let's review a scripture that has popped up frequently throughout our study. Colossians 3:12 reminds us that we are *holy, chosen, and dearly loved* by our heavenly Father.

If this truth has been hidden, twisted, or taken from you, you will most likely search somewhere else to fill the hole in your soul that craves worth, love, and fulfillment. If God is not the primary source of molding, shaping, and filling your life, you will search for other temporary and not-so-satisfying alternatives.

There are many places and things to which we can run for fulfillment. Many women expend a lot of energy chasing relationships, careers, wealth, and material possessions in hopes of finding fulfillment. While these things may bring pleasure and greatly enrich our lives, they cannot sustain you as Jesus does.

The writer of Hebrews reminds us of this in Hebrews 7, *"Therefore he is able to save completely those who come to God through him, because he always lives to intercede for them. ²⁶ Such a high priest truly meets our need—one who is holy, blameless, pure, set apart from sinners, exalted above the heavens."* Hebrews 7:25-26

Only Jesus can meet every need you have. Only Jesus can satisfy every longing in your heart. Only Jesus can heal every hurt and restore every wound. Only Jesus knows you intimately and thoroughly. Only Jesus is perfectly holy, blameless, pure, and without sin. Only Jesus loves you with perfect, unselfish, unconditional love. And only Jesus died for you to take away your sin so you could be reconciled to God, enjoy a relationship with Him, and be restored to the fullness in which God created you to live.

When my kids were little, it was an indulgence for us to allow them to drink soda with their meals. It was such a big treat that they couldn't decide which flavor they wanted. To satisfy their indecision, they would fill their cups with a little bit of every kind of soda available at the fountain. They thought it tasted great, but I had trouble distinguishing any distinct flavor because they were all mixed together.

Too often, our lives resemble these soda drinks. We're filled with a little bit of everything – every kind of lifestyle and attitude – leaving the true flavor of Christ diluted, overpowered, or completely indistinguishable, which won't quench our thirst or satisfy our souls.

God can only fill our lives to the extent that we empty ourselves and allow Him to fill us. The Holy Spirit, alive and active in us, never leaves us empty or wanting for more. He is the only Person who will truly meet our need for reconciliation and forgiveness, and He is the only Person who will fill and satisfy your soul.

Day Two – Wabi-sabi

The Japanese have a design concept called *Wabi-sabi* that discovers beauty in the imperfect and incomplete. This centuries-old design idea embraces the awareness that life is fragile and constantly changing.

Wabi-sabi acknowledges the chaos of everyday life and the flaws we so often try to conceal and instead says, "Yes, I see loveliness there too."[1] (How I needed to hear this when I had a house filled with toddlers!)

Aspiring to live the *Wabi-sabi* philosophy inspires you to live authentically, surrounding yourself with items that reflect the fullness of who you really are. The challenge, though, is that this inevitably requires our willingness to receive less-than-perfect things into our lives.

What a great way to approach life – to find beauty in the perfectly imperfect. Contentment amid chaos. No filters over our flaws. Finding joy despite loose ends and unanswered questions.

Being at peace with the constant tension between what's *beautiful* about us and, at the same time, accepting the *brokenness* of who we truly are, frees us to be the best version of ourselves. We're content right where we're at, yet at the same time pressing forward to fill our lives with more of God's presence and Christ's likeness.

In Christ, we are full; we are free. Free from depending on ourselves for salvation. Free from feeling driven to be loved and accepted. Free from the cycle of failure and despair.

As the apostle Paul wrote in Romans, *"...through Christ Jesus the law of the Spirit of life set me free from the law of sin and death."* Romans 8:2

I spent years staring at the Law, feeling overwhelmed, guilty, and like a failure. The harder I determined to work, the more my time with Jesus became a rigid outline of what I thought was expected of me instead of a life-giving relationship.

God desires to live a full life overflowing with His love, grace, and presence. He longs to empower our lives with His presence, to restore and heal our souls and fill the empty longing in our hearts. But He can only begin to do that when we empty ourselves, humble our hearts and ask Him to fill our lives.

In Christ, God gives us what we didn't deserve but what we desperately needed. He didn't demand perfection, just a desire to be with Him.

If you're a parent, you get this. I didn't have five children so that they could do things for me. My children bring me joy by simply being themselves. Every day I marvel at their uniqueness. Every day I love them, care for them, and desire to bless them—not because I am hoping for something in return, but because my love for them is so great.

How much more does our perfect heavenly Father love you? Everything we have to offer Him pales in comparison to what God has done for us and offers to us.

You give God pleasure simply because of who you are. God created you uniquely—different from anybody else. You have special gifts, interests, and abilities. He doesn't love you *if* you behave and obey, or *because* you're successful and beautiful, or *when* you go to church and read your Bible.

His grace can't be earned; it is freely given. His grace is the absolute, undeserved, unmerited love and favor of a lavish God who requires nothing in return.

This used to be hard for me to understand. I tried to obey all the rules. I craved intimacy with God and others but lacked the authenticity essential for a real relationship.

When people saw my weaknesses, I was devastated and felt like a failure. The closer people got to me, the more pronounced my many flaws became, so I determined to be less vulnerable and work harder to keep up the appearance of having it all together.

In my twisted thinking, I thought if I kept people at a distance, they wouldn't see my needs; they wouldn't see my flaws. What an unsatisfying, unfulfilling way to live! I wasn't being changed, and I wasn't maturing. And even more tragic, my relationships lacked a depth that I craved but was terrified to explore.

I wasn't relying on God's grace; I was trying to protect myself. Instead of asking God to fill me (*wabi-sabi* and all) with the fullness of who He is, I protected my heart. In doing so, I kept close relationships at bay and limited the work God desired to do in me.

Wabi-sabi, my friend. There's no need to cover up your faults and exhaust yourself trying to achieve perfection. Embrace the beauty in your brokenness...admire the imperfect in your everyday life. Allow Him to remove the filters and expose the rough edges as He molds you into the woman He has created you to be. God wants to fill your life. But you must take the first step to open your heart.

Day Three – Growing Up

When my girls were little, they loved playing dress-up by wearing my clothes and shoes (and yes, they would get into my *wip gwoss*, too). Yet, you would never mistake them for an adult woman. They looked like little girls playing dress-up. It took years for them to grow into the beautiful young women they are today.

Similarly, maturity in Christ isn't something we obtain instantaneously. It's not something we can fake or pretend to have. It's developed in our lives through the process of growth.

And growth takes time. The Madagascar palm is said to grow slowly and steadily – sometimes for 10 or 15 years – before it even begins to bloom!

Be patient with yourself. Your walk with God won't bloom overnight. Growth is a slow process that happens when we choose to live for God every day, work through conflicts, wrestle through relationships, allow His Spirit to shape and fashion our life, and learn to embrace every season in which we find ourselves…even the difficult and uncomfortable ones.

In the book of James, we're instructed that the result of our suffering through trials is maturity and completeness. The idea that

292

God grows and matures us through suffering isn't the "good news" we hope to hear when we read God's Word. We want a quick fix, an easy road to growth, but James is clear.

"Consider it pure joy, my brothers and sisters, whenever you face trials of many kinds, ³ because you know that the testing of your faith produces perseverance. ⁴ Let perseverance finish its work so that you may be mature and complete, not lacking anything." James 1:3-5

I wish there were easier ways for God to "finish" His work in my life, but time after time, the result of maturity has required a measure of my personal blood, sweat, and tears.

While we all desire maturity and completeness, we don't always like the path that will get us there. To avoid discomfort and pain, we often attempt to shortcut the work of God, dressing up our "outside lives" while avoiding the work and perseverance necessary to build our character and mature our faith.

No one can build your character for you. You can read books about character, study, and research it, and compile a lot of information about it, but at some point, you must partner with God and build it by digging deep into your soul.

Asking the right people to speak into your life is important. Small group community, being a part of a church, and having people pray for you will encourage you and give you strength, but they cannot build your character. They cannot persevere for you.

Only you can do that, and you must work at it if you want to grow in Christ.

Perseverance is that strength inside of you that allows you to push through the pain to get to a place where you look back and realize there was an inner strength you didn't know you had. Perseverance is choosing to keep going even when you don't think you can. On the other side of perseverance, you realize that you can do hard things!

Moms, you know about perseverance. When you're sick, the kids still need you. You don't get to sleep in or take a day off. You keep going.

If you're a student, you're learning the value of perseverance. (If you don't, you won't be in school for long!) You study and sometimes pull all-nighters to get the work done. Every time you choose to turn off the TV and crack open the books, you're building inner strength.

If you're working, you've experienced this too. You show up to work on time and do your job well. If every day's a vacation day, the work will pile up, and pretty soon, you won't have a job. So, you persevere. You push through.

We all have had to learn some level of perseverance. Life doesn't stop when you're going through a difficult season. Through the trials, through the pain, through the discomfort, God is building something in you. Don't give up, even in your pain. Cling to God... Tap into His power... Keep showing up. Keep fighting. Stay connected to your small group. Keep getting out of bed. Make the drive to church. Continue reading your Bible.

And you know what you'll find? You'll discover, as James tells us, that perseverance does something inside of us. It makes us mature and complete.

You can hire a personal trainer at the gym, but eventually, you must lift the weights to build your muscle mass. As you build muscle, you become stronger. And when you get to the other side of your pain and didn't give up, you realize you're stronger than before. There's a deeper resilience in you.

Your character is strengthened, and your faith is stronger. God got you through something you didn't think you could endure, but you've now experienced His faithfulness.

The fruits of the Spirit are more evident in your life. You're kinder, more compassionate, wiser, and more patient. There's greater peace in your heart because God has carried you through something and built something in you.

But you had to work for it.

Maturity and completeness. To be so content in our souls that we seek nothing else. We're completely satisfied by God. Isn't that something we all desire?

But it's not free. You must push through the pain to receive it. You'll be so glad you did.

Day Four – Pools of 'Ohe'o

On the island of Maui, just past the quaint town of Hana, you will find the *Pools of 'Ohe'o*, also known as the seven sacred pools. Nestled in a serene tropical environment, this series of waterfalls, streams, and pools crafted by lava beds begins nearly two miles inland, gradually making its way to its final destination, emptying into the Pacific Ocean. Centuries of rainfall have carved these pools into the lava rocks. Beginning high in the sky, unseen and blanketed by the clouds, rainfall fills the first pool, spilling over into the second pool, which then overflows into another…and another…and another, pouring the fresh-water rain into the salty sea.

If you've made it to this point in our study, I pray that God has done some growth and refining in your heart. I know He's done that in mine. As we empty ourselves of our "old self", cluttered by fear, rejection, shame, and insecurity, we create more space for God's refreshing presence and character to fill our lives.

Think of these *Pools of 'Ohe'o* as representing the fullness of the life God has. As He fills us, the overflow of His presence in our life spills into every other "pool".

God desires to first fill us with Himself. He does this as we spend time with Him throughout the day, as we empty ourselves to Him. The natural outflow of His fullness in our life "spills" into the lives of those around us—our husbands, our children, our family, friends, and co-workers…to a broken world that is empty, dry, and thirsting for hope, purpose, and significance.

But what would happen if there was no inflow? No rainfall to fill these pools? We'd only see dry riverbeds sitting amid parched foliage. The inflow of rainfall at the 'Ohe'o pools provides vitality, growth, and health to the area.

If God doesn't fill our lives with His presence, what will we have to pour out to others? It will most likely be the stuff we work so hard to keep hidden. Impatience, anger, frustration, fear, complaining, and worry will be our natural default if we're not receiving a fresh inflow of God's presence.

In John 10:10, Jesus describes the life He has for you, "*The thief comes only to steal and kill and destroy; I have come that they may have life, and have it to the full.*" John 10:10

God created you for a full life. Not a busy life, filled with activity. It's filled with the presence of God. The word, *full*, in this verse, comes from the Greek word *perisson*, meaning superabundant, over and above, more than enough.

This kind of *fullness* describes the life God created for you to enjoy. Where we are lacking, He supplies more than enough. It doesn't mean your life will be absent of difficulties or conflicts, but it does mean that your circumstances shouldn't control your life or prevent you from experiencing the abundance of God's peace, contentment, joy, and abundance.

In Colossians 2, Paul explains this amazing thing that happens to us when we choose to follow Jesus. *"For in Christ all the fullness of the Deity lives in bodily form, [10] and in Christ you have been brought to fullness. He is the head over every power and authority."* Colossians 2:9-10

Christ is God in human form. He's not part god or kind of god, but fully God. Everything that God is – His goodness, grace, faithfulness, power – was found in its perfection and completeness in Christ. Paul is now declaring that the same power dwells in us.

When Christ fills our life, we are complete. The emptiness that once existed dissipates, and we are filled with the same Spirit that Jesus possessed when He lived on earth. The Spirit of God, who is head over every power and authority, lives inside those who have received Jesus as Lord. Amazing, right?!

Throughout the New Testament, Christ is described as filling everything in every way. Words cannot begin to accurately express the immensity of God's fullness. Dear friend, we serve a massive, abundant God, yet He is so intimately concerned and personally connected to His children that not one of your needs goes unmet, not one tear you cry goes unbottled, and not one hair of your head goes unnumbered.

God has so much for you! He has given you a full, abundant life through a relationship with Him. It is for a special purpose: *to be poured out in service to a broken world.*

God's Spirit living in you has the power and potential for luxurious growth even in what appears to be dry surroundings. Like the *Pools of 'Ohe'o*, God desires to use the fullness He has given you to fill others and see them reconciled to God.

God gave us His only Son, who emptied Himself in service to us, so we could experience a relationship with Him. Out of love and gratitude, shouldn't we aspire to do likewise?

Day Five – What is Real?

Well, this is it, my friend. Our time together is ending. I'm so proud of the investment you've made these past few weeks to do some honest soul work. I pray you've allowed God into some of the hidden places in your heart, and, as a result, He's been able to shape and mold you to better reflect the image of Christ and who He created you to be.

The neat thing about becoming the beautiful woman God created is that you can totally achieve it! You have exactly what it takes! You don't have to strive to be something you're not. You don't have to pretend you're capable or talented in areas where you're not gifted. God gets the greatest delight and glory when you're the best at being you!

As you continue this never-ending journey of becoming like Christ, remember to keep your eyes on Jesus. He's the One we're chasing. We get off track when our focus shifts, and we start chasing other people or things.

As Bob Goff writes, "We'll never be like Jesus if it's more important for us to be like each other. Stack up all the pressure you're feeling to be something different and ask yourself whether the image looks like Jesus. If it does, you're moving in the right direction."[3]

That's some good advice. Amid the myriad of options and opinions, only One opinion matters. Don't compare your everyday life to someone else's filtered and edited one. God never compares His creation, and neither should you. As you run wholeheartedly in that direction, God will shape you into the most authentic version of yourself.

We've learned during these past few weeks that being real and authentic doesn't mean perfect and flawless.

In the cherished children's book, *The Velveteen Rabbit*, the rabbit and the horse discuss this,

"What is REAL?" asked the Rabbit one day... "Does it mean having things that buzz inside you and a stick-out handle?"
"Real isn't how you are made," said the Skin Horse. "It's a thing that happens to you. When a child loves you for a long, long time, not just to play with, but REALLY loves you, then you become Real."
"Does it hurt?" asked the Rabbit.
"Sometimes," said the Skin Horse, for he was always

truthful. "When you are Real you don't mind being hurt."

"Does it happen all at once, like being wound up," he asked, "or bit by bit?"

"It doesn't happen all at once," said the Skin Horse. "You become. It takes a long time. That's why it doesn't happen often to people who break easily, or have sharp edges, or who have to be carefully kept. Generally, by the time you are Real, most of your hair has been loved off, and your eyes drop out and you get loose in the joints and very shabby. But these things don't matter at all, because once you are Real you can't be ugly, except to people who don't understand." [4]

If you're feeling worn and shabby, take heart. God is doing something spectacular inside of you. And remember, it's not just for you – He wants you to share His love with a world that has yet to experience it.

But as C.S. Lewis explained, "Your real new self…will not come as long as you are looking for it. It will come when you are looking for Him." [5]

As we look to Him, God not only shapes us into the people He created us to be, He gives us an abundance of His grace freely flowing through our lives, demonstrating His goodness to a creation that longs and looks for it elsewhere.

Let's look at one last scripture passage. I especially love how John describes the fullness of God's grace, *"Yet to all who did receive him, to those who believed in his name, he gave the right to become children of God—* ¹³ *children born not of natural descent, nor of human decision or a husband's will, but born of God.* ¹⁴ *The Word became flesh and made his dwelling among us. We have seen his glory, the glory of the one and only Son, who came from the Father, full of grace and truth."* John 1:12-14

The fullness of God's grace and truth aren't received through our achievements or accomplishments. It's a gift God gives to those whose hearts are open to receiving it.

John continues embellishing this thought through verse 16, *"Out of his fullness we have all received grace in place of grace already given."* John 1:16

I'm so grateful for God's abundant grace. His grace is not weak; it empowers us to live out our calling from God.

The original Greek word for *grace* in these verses is *charis*, meaning "that which causes joy, pleasure, gratification, favor, and acceptance . . . A favor done without expectation of return, the absolute free expression of the loving kindness of God to men, finding its only motive in the bounty and benevolence of the Giver; unearned and unmerited favor . . .. It is the direct antithesis to the Greek word *erga*, which means work.⁶

As we close our time together, lean into this thought.

When your life is falling apart – His grace is enough.

When your emotions are out of control – His grace is enough.

When you're weary and sleep-deprived – His grace is enough.

When you're frustrated and discouraged – His grace is enough.

When you're overworked and overwhelmed – His grace is enough.

When you're criticized and condemned – His grace is enough.

When insecurity and rejection arise – His grace is enough.

Dear friend, His grace is enough to fill every crack in your broken heart. His grace is enough to fill the void of loneliness. His grace is enough to provide hope when you're hurting.

God's grace, out of His fullness, is overflowing, abundant, and ready to fill your heart with even more grace.

Just *as a face is reflected in water, so the heart reflects the real person (Proverbs 27:19 NLT).* You are chosen, holy, and dearly loved just as you are. Believe it. Embrace it. Pursue it. Aloha.

Thank you...

Where do I even begin? Just about everything I do is the result of a team effort. This devotional is no exception. So many people have invested in my life through the years. Each experience, every word, and all the prayers have shaped me into the woman I am today. I am incredibly grateful.

Thank you, dear reader, for allowing me to share my thoughts and stories with you. I'm honored to have walked with you these past few weeks and humbled that you gave me the opportunity to speak to some tender areas.

Gregg, thank you for being my best friend and standing by my side. There's no one else with whom I'd want to share this wild adventure. You've made the rough seasons bearable and the good seasons even better. You're my companion, my confidant, my cheerleader, and my forever love. I love you with all my heart.

Rebecca, Brandon, Justin, Jordan, and Jessica, thank you for being my tribe. You are my favorite people in the entire world. Being your mom is my greatest joy and accomplishment. I'm so proud of the men and women you're becoming. I love you, and I believe you will change the world.

Our parents, thank you for giving us the example of a loving marriage and lives that love Jesus. I always treasure our time together, and even though we live scattered across the country, you always support and encourage us. I love you dearly.

Pastor Norman and Faye Nakanishi, thank you for believing in us, mentoring us, and being a safe place for us. Pastor Norman, you are the only man I know who would so graciously accept the request to write an introduction to a women's devotional.

Deborah and my PW squad (you know who you are), thank you for showing up every month. I cherish your friendship, learn from your wisdom, and am stretched by your faith.

Grace Honolulu, thank you for allowing us to be a small part of what God is doing to transform lives in Hawaii. Gregg and I are so incredibly thankful God has called us to serve alongside you.

Endnotes

Chapter One

1. Blueletterbible.org, David Guzik commentary, "Study Guide for Ephesians 3."
2. Henri J.M. Nouwen, *The Life of the Beloved* (Canada: The Crossroad Publishing Company, 1992), 45.

Chapter Two

1. Soren Kierkegaard, as quoted by John Ortberg, *The Life You've Always Wanted* (Grand Rapids: Zondervan, 1997, 2002), 11.

Chapter Three

1. Hans Christen Andersen, *The Ugly Duckling* (Originally published in 1843).
2. Dizzy Dean: https://baseballhall.org/hall-of-famers/dean-dizzy. I originally heard this story at the *Leading and Loving It* retreat during a breakout session led by Dr. Charity Byers.
3. Spiros Zodhaites, *The Complete Word Study Dictionary: New Testament* (Chattanooga: AMG Publishers, 1992), 478 & Strong's Concordance.
4. NIV Study Bible (Zondervan), notes from Colossians 3:1.
5. Bob Goff, *Everybody Always* (Nelson Books: 2018), 66.
6. Carly Fiorina quoting something her mother would tell her. From the "Craig Groeschel Leadership Podcast", episode 56.
7. Zodhaites, *The Complete Word Study Dictionary: New Testament* (Chattanooga: AMG Publishers, 1992), 968.
8. Stormie Omartian, *Lord, I Want to Be Whole* (Nashville: Thomas Nelson Publishers, 2000), 78.

Chapter Four

1. Bibletools.org, *Greek/Hebrew Definitions, hamartano*. Strong's #264.
2. Rice Broocks, Engage 2020: "Igniting a Missional Movement" seminar (Seminar manual, April 2014), 4.
3. John Ortberg, *Everybody's Normal Till You Get to Know Them* (Grand Rapids: Zondervan, 2003), 206-207.
4. En, Strong's Concordance: Greek, 1722.
5. Max Lucado, *Facing Your Giants* (Nashville: W Publishing Group, 2006), 50.

Chapter Five
1. Taylor Swift, *Mean* (Produced by Taylor Swift and Nathan Chapman, on the album Speak Now, 2011).
2. Shauna Niequist, *Savor*, (Grand Rapids: Zondervan, 2015), 308.

Chapter 6
1. Book of Hosea, Old Testament, Chapters 1-3.
2. Tim Keller, *The Meaning of Marriage* (New York: Penguin Books, 2011), 164.
3. J. I. Packer, *Knowing God* (Downers Grove: InterVarsity Press, 1973), 123.
4. Strong's Concordance, G5278, hupomeno.
5. W.E. Vine, *Vine's Expository Dictionary of Biblical Words* (Nashville: Thomas Nelson Publishers, 1985), 382.
6. Hannah Whitall Smith, as quoted in *Lies Women Believe and the Truth that Sets Them Free* (Chicago: Moody Press, 2001), 52.

Chapter 7 endnotes
1. https://www.pbs.org/wgbh/roadshow/season/2/secaucus-nj/appraisals/seymour-card-table-ca-1794--199708A13/.

Chapter 8 endnotes
2. David Guzik, *Blue Letter Bible Online Commentary*, Study notes for Luke 6.
3. John Calvin, *The Crossway Classic Commentaries: Isaiah* (Wheaton: Crossway Books, 2000), 395.
4. https://www.sheknows.com/entertainment/articles/984055/model-cameron-russell-reveals-industrys-insecurities/.

Chapter 9 endnotes
1. Joyce Meyer, *Approval Addiction*, (Faith Words Publishing, 2008).
2. John Ortberg, *Love Beyond Reason* (Grand Rapids: Zondervan, 1998), 49-51.
3. Lysa Terkeurst, *Uninvited* (Nashville: Nelson Books, 2016), 21.
4. Lori Wilhite, *My Name is Victorious*, (USA: Leading and Loving It, 2017), 75.
5. Matt Clifford and Mick Jagger, *Dancing in the Street*, Performed by David Bowie and Mick Jagger (1985, Warner/Chappell Music, Inc, BMG Rights Management).
6. Tyrkeurst, *Uninvited*, 30.

Chapter 10 endnotes
1. Erwin McManus, *The Last Arrow* (Colorado Springs: WaterBrook, 2017), 134.

Chapter 11 endnotes
1. Elizabeth Elliot, *Passion and Purity* (Grand Rapids: Revell, 1984), 131-32.
2. Dallas Willard, *Renovation of the Heart*, as quoted by John Ortberg in Soul Keeping (Grand Rapids: Zondervan, 2014), 15.
3. Lori Wilhite, *My Name is Victorious* (Henderson: Leading and Loving It, 2017), 119.
4. Craig Groeschel, sermon titled, *Complaining; Me and My Big Mouth*, open.life.church/resources/3312-my-big-fat-mouth?search_id=17325838.
5. Originally read about this art form in Lori Wilhite's book, *My Name is Victorious*, 26. The research I did to describe this amazing form of art can be found at: mymodernmet.com/kintsugi-kintsukuroi/.

Chapter 12 endnotes
1. Stephen Seamands, *Ministry in the Image of God*, (Downers Grove: InterVarsity Press, 2005), 92.
2. AA Milne, *Winnie the Pooh*, well-known quote from the book.
3. nytimes.com/2018/01/17/world/europe/uk-britain-loneliness.html, *UK Appoints a Minister for Loneliness*, 01/17/2018.
4. Multiple sources were used in my research on the Feast of Booths: Ligonier.org, David Guzik's commentary on John, and NT Wright's commentary on John.

Chapter 13 endnotes
1. John Mark Comer, *The Ruthless Elimination of Hurry* (Colorado Springs: Water Brook, 2019), 55.
2. https://www.goodreads.com/quotes/655841-if-the-devil-cannot-make-us-bad-he-will-make.
3. Jennie Allen, *Get Out of Your Head* (USA: Waterbrook, 2020), 10.
4. www.biography.com/activist/harriet-tubman.
5. Eric Liddell, taken from Eric Liddell's book, *The Disciplines of the Christian Life*, (London: SPCK Publishing, 2009) as quoted by Kay Warren during the 2020 Just One conference.

Chapter 14 endnotes

1. https://www.nationalgeographic.com/news/2015/07/150720-shark-attack-surfer-mick-fanning-south-africa/.
2. Beth Moore, *Believing God* (Nashville: Broadman and Holman Publishers, 2004), 10.
3. https://www.olympic.org/lasse-viren.

Chapter 15 endnotes

1. Lee Grady, *www.charismamag.com* "Fire in My Bones", July 7, 2010.
2. Magnolia Journal, issue 12. Fall 2019, 71.
3. Bob Goff, *Live in Grace, Walk in Love* (Nashville: Nelson Books, 2019), 292.
4. Marjorie Williams Bianco, a well-known quote from *The Velveteen Rabbit*
5. C.S. Lewis, *Mere Christianity* (New York: MacMillan, 1960) p. 190. As quoted by Stephen Seamands, Ministry in the Image of God (Downers Grove: InterVarsity Press, 2005), 133.
6. Zohadites, *The Complete Word Study Dictionary (Chattanooga: AMG Publishers*, 1992), 1469.